31-43

THE DEAD SEA SCROLLS AND THE BIBLE

The
Dead Sea Scrolls
and the Bible

by

ROLAND E. MURPHY, O. CARM.

Professor of Old Testament
The Catholic University of America

68899

BM
487
.M97

The Newman Press · Westminster, Maryland

1965

Imprimi potest: Very Rev. Raphael P. Kieffer, O.Carm.
                  Prior Provincialis

Nihil obstat: Edward S. Cerny, S.S., D.D.
                  Censor Librorum

Imprimatur: †Francis P. Keough, D.D.
                  Archbishop of Baltimore

August 13, 1956

The *nihil obstat* and *imprimatur* are official declarations that a book or pamphlet is free of doctrinal and moral error. No implication is contained therein that those who have granted the *nihil obstat* and *imprimatur* agree with the opinions expressed.

First published 1956

Second printing 1957

Third printing 1961

Fourth printing 1963

Fifth printing 1965

Contents

Introduction

At least two hazards await all who write or read about the famous Dead Sea scrolls and fragments. The first is the fact that not all of the Dead Sea material has been published and made available to students. From the present booklet the reader will understand why this is so. Nevertheless, what has been published thus far has been diligently studied by various scholars of all shades of opinion. The constant give and take in these scholarly debates has been profitable: certain facts have been established, conclusions are beginning to emerge; one may say that the path of future study of the scrolls has been charted.

The second hazard is harder to cope with than the first, but it offers exciting possibilities. This is the continuing probability of more discoveries. At the present time it is known that a new cave, called Cave 11, has been discovered in connection with the campaign at Khirbet Qumran in the spring of this year. This cave, situated slightly north of Qumran, was discovered and looted by the Bedouin. By the time the archeologists got to it, only a few fragments could be found. Reports issuing from Palestine indicate that several scrolls, more or less complete, were taken from this cave, and responsible archeologists are in contact with the Bedouin about them. While no official identification of these scrolls has been published at this writing, the contents of Cave 11 put one in mind of the startling finds of Cave 1 (discovered in 1947), since there are several continuous pieces, and not merely fragments.

Despite these hazards, the reader will find enough factual information in this booklet to put the scrolls and fragments in their proper perspective. We have omitted many difficult questions concerning the identification, history and practices of the ancient people to whom the newly found documents belonged. These are largely questions of academic interest. Rather, the purpose of this booklet is to introduce the reader to the story of the scrolls, their finding and their bearing on the Bible. For the average reader, it is in this religious sphere that the main interest of the scrolls lies. Do the scrolls contribute to our understanding of the Bible? Most certainly. Gaps in our knowledge of the history of the transmission of the Old Testament text have been filled, and we have a new understanding of the Palestinian background in which the Gospel of Jesus Christ was preached. This booklet intends to illustrate these two points by frequent references to the texts of the scrolls and of the New Testament. The reader will not fail to be impressed by the modernity of the Christian message for its first audience; it was expressed in the religious terminology and ideas of Jesus' contemporaries. By the same token, the reader will not be fooled by the hasty and ill-conceived claims of some recent writers. Christianity does not "derive" from the ancient Jewish sect that treasured these newly found scrolls. However, the popular exaggerations about the connection between Christianity and the sect of the scrolls have not been without fruit; the scrolls have been studied ever more diligently, and on all sides a need for careful, balanced judgment has been felt.

Specialists will recognize in this booklet the

fruit of various studies by Albright, Skehan, Cross, De Vaux, Barthelemy and many others. Many of the conclusions have appeared in scholarly journals such as the *Revue Biblique*, the *Bulletin of the American Schools of Oriental Research*, the *Journal of Biblical Literature*, the *Catholic Biblical Quarterly*, etc. Perhaps the most heartening feature in the story of the scrolls has been the close collaboration of scholars of various races and religions in the work of deciphering, publishing and studying the scrolls. Without their dedicated work it would not be possible to provide the reader with the new insights into the Bible which the scrolls afford.

ROLAND E. MURPHY, O. Carm.
The Catholic University of America
August 22, 1956

List of Illustrations

ABBREVIATIONS

Chapter 1

The Discovery of Ancient Scrolls and Fragments

1947–1950: the Dead Sea Scrolls

Every one who travels in Palestine is impressed by the bleak, rugged terrain. It is rocky, sparsely seeded, devoid of the rich loam of other countries. Even the occasional oasis created by a well or river-bed, as at Jericho, serves only to heighten the general impression of dry barrenness. The Judean desert to the northwest of the Dead Sea is a prime example of such wilderness. Yet this hilly region, so uninviting to us now, was a refuge to David in his outlaw days and to John the Baptist during the preparation for his mission as Precursor to Jesus. In early Christian times it had a surprising number of foundations, such as the famous Mar Saba monastery which still exists. Today the wilderness is home for the semi-nomadic Arab tribes; they camp in their black goatskin tents, as well as in the many caves of the region, but always near a water source. It was near such a water source, the Wadi Qumran, that the ten caves which have yielded the famous Dead Sea Scrolls and fragments were discovered.

In the Spring of 1947 a young Palestinian goatherd, with the realistic name of Muhammed adh-Dhib ("the wolf"), accidentally discovered Cave 1. He gathered some of his fellows of the Taamireh tribe and set off for Bethlehem to sell the old leather scrolls he had found. These Bedouin were free of the disadvantages that later sceptical scholars labored under; these scrolls looked old and even smelled old, under their linen wrappings. Although the young men were not able to read the archeological significance of the tall jars in which they found the scrolls preserved, they were alert to the possibilities of trading. But the Bethlehem merchants were not impressed. One offered £20; another referred them to his religious superior, Mar Yeshue Samuel, the Syrian Archbishop at St. Mark's Monastery in Jerusalem. The Arabs made their trip to the north, only to be refused admittance at the Syrian monastery! When the Archbishop finally contacted them, one had already taken his share elsewhere, and these particular scrolls were eventually sold to the famous Jewish archeologist, the late E. L. Sukenik. But Mar Yeshue Samuel, without knowing their full value, secured the rest for a reported $150.

This was in July, 1947, and an amusing, if understandable, story of incredulity began. No one could quite believe that the Archbishop's scrolls were ancient. True, one of the scrolls was recognized as a copy of the book of Isaias, but it was too much to expect that any manuscript should have survived in Palestine from an early age. The corrosion worked by weather and time would seem to preclude such a possibility. Mar Yeshue Samuel found little encouragement from those he approached for a judgment on his manuscripts. Some of his friends made contact with Professor Sukenik, despite the ominous signs of the civil war that was soon to break out between Israelis and Arabs. Sukenik had recognized the value of the scrolls he had already acquired and was anxious to purchase the group belonging to the Archbishop. But before negotiations were completed, Mar Yeshue Samuel had recourse to the American School of Oriental Research in Jerusalem during February, 1948. The Americans were of the opinion that his scrolls were genuinely ancient and sent a photographic sample to Professor William F. Albright, the world-renowned Semitist and archeologist of Johns Hopkins University, who confirmed their judgment.

Thus it turned out that the scrolls of Cave 1 became separated and were eventually published by different parties. Professor Sukenik's lot included three documents: the incomplete Isaias text, the Thanksgiving Psalms, and the War between the Children of Light and the Children of Darkness. The Syrian Archbishop's acquisition counted four works: the complete text of Isaias, the Habacuc commentary, and the Manual of Discipline. The fourth document, the so-called "Lamech" scroll, only recently unrolled, has now been recognized as an Aramaic paraphrase of certain chapters of Genesis. All these scrolls are now in the hands of the Government of Israel, since the Archbishop sold his lot to Israel indirectly, for the sum of $250,000. On February 13, 1955, Moshe Sharret, Israel's foreign minister, announced that the scrolls would be housed in a special "Shrine of the Book."

The 1947 discovery shook the scholarly world and studies of the scrolls quickly appeared. Controversy began concerning the age of these documents, and there was even the charge of a "hoax." But thanks to scientific method, all reasonable doubt about the genuinity of the scrolls has been dispelled. There are now three principal means available for dating: the tried and tested method of pottery study, the somewhat less certain means of paleography (study of style of writing), and the newly discovered carbon 14 process.

Since the work of the great English archeologist, Sir Flinders Petrie, at the beginning of the twentieth century, pottery has become the key by which the archeologist opens up the historical periods of the past. To the trained eye, the shape, ware, color and other characteristics of a given jar spell out its age. Using this "ceramic index," the excavators determined that the several whole jars which contained the scrolls, along with the jar fragments which were found, belonged to the first century B.C.

The carbon 14 process, developed by Dr. W. F. Libby at the Institute for Nuclear Studies of the University of Chicago, has only recently been at the service of archeologists. Carbon 14 is a radioactive form of carbon (atomic weight 14) which is present in all organic matter. By measuring its rate of decay, the age of the organic matter can be judged. Dr. Libby applied his test to the linen wrappings in which the scrolls had been found and obtained the date 33 A.D., plus or minus 200. The margin of error, therefore, allowed of a date between 167 B.C., and 233 A.D. Libby's dates received further confirmation from a radiocarbon count conducted by the Carnegie Institute of Technology. This test dated the linen wrappings found in Cave 1 to about 50 A.D. as the latest possible date.

The third criterion used for judging the age of the scrolls was paleography, the study of the writing forms and styles used by the copyists. Like pottery, handwriting also has its distinctive characteristics. If we have enough samples over a given period, we can trace the development in the forms of the letters. If some of the samples are dated, a careful comparison can yield the approximate date of the rest. On this basis, the specialists in Hebrew paleography set to work on the scrolls and fragments. They would have wished for more samples from sources other than the caves for the purposes of comparison, but they were fortunate enough to be presented with dated Hebrew documents from the first and second century A.D. (found in the Wadi Murabbaat in 1952), the script of which shows a development that is demonstrably later than those of the Cave 1 scrolls. While one allows for the necessarily general nature of a conclusion based on forms of letters, one must still admit that this evidence has confirmed the first impressions concerning the age of the scrolls when they were brought to the American School of Oriental Research in 1948.

Despite these strong arguments proving the antiquity of the scrolls, there remained a bit of uneasiness as long as one question remained unanswered: how did the scrolls get into the cave in the first place? Once the scrolls were tied in with a definite group of people who used them, there would be even greater certainty about their antiquity. The answer to this problem touched off a whole series of new discoveries that went beyond an archeologist's wildest dreams: the excavation of the "monastery" at Qumran.

1951–1956: the "Monastery" and the Caves

The ruins (Khirbet) of Qumran are the remnants of an ancient building located on a ridge in the high mountain cliffs at the northwest end of the Dead Sea. Situated only about a half-mile to the south of Cave 1, this site had been inspected by the archeologists in 1949, but no large-scale digging was done. At the end of 1951, Father Roland de Vaux, O.P., director of the famous *École Biblique* in Jerusalem, and G. L. Harding, director of the Department of Antiquities in Jordan, opened the first of a series of five campaigns (the last in March, 1956), and the secret of the scrolls began to unfold.

The ruins turned out to be a community center or, as it is now popularly called, a "monastery." The most important feature of the building was that it was *not* a dwelling place, but a place of assembly for meetings, study, writing, and eating. The community itself lived in the hundreds of nearby caves and in tents, but repaired to the monastery for their communal activities. The building is rectangular in shape, measuring about 100 by 120 feet, built of large, undressed stones. A huge two-story tower, forty feet square, with walls five feet thick that had been split by an earthquake, still dominates the ruins, standing to a height of about fifteen feet. Several large rooms—too large for a private dwelling—which served as kitchens and store rooms, have been cleared away. One room with a bench along the walls has been suggested as the council room. The largest single room is a little over 70 feet long and has at one end the remnants of what is conjectured to be a lectern base; this room may have served as a refectory or assembly hall. Adjoining it is a store room that was found still equipped with hundreds of jars and dishes. On the second floor of another building unit (which had fallen through when the archeologists discovered it) was located the *scriptorium*, with brick and plaster tables where the members doubtlessly copied out several of the scrolls which were later deposited in the recently discovered caves. There were even three inkwells discovered in the ruins of this room. The pottery establishment found at Qumran is one of the best preserved in Palestine. A dozen pools and cisterns, some of them with steps, underline the emphasis which the scrolls lay on lustrations and washings.

Thanks to strict archeological method, the following picture can be reconstructed. The presence of particular types of pottery and coins indicate that the monastery was occupied from a period shortly before 100 B.C., down to the time of the First Jewish Revolt against Rome about 70 A.D. This period of occupation had been interrupted about 31 B.C., which is the date of an earthquake mentioned by the Jewish historian, Josephus. Since there is only one coin from the reign of Herod the Great (37–4 B.C.), it appears that the building was abandoned at this time. But community life was resumed again at the beginning of the Christian era until the crushing defeat of the Jews by Vespasian's army put an end to the settlement at Qumran. After 70 A.D., there are no signs of community life; there is evidence of the Roman military (iron arrowheads of the Roman legion) and a few Jewish insurgents under Bar Kochba who utilised the site shortly before the Second Jewish Revolt of 135 A.D.

The discovery of the Qumran monastery gave the most reasonable explanation of the presence of the scrolls in the caves. The pottery found at the monastery matches the pottery found in the caves. The history of the main building suggests that shortly before the advance of the Roman legions during the First Jewish Revolt, the community hid their sacred writings in the numerous caves in the area. They wrapped the scrolls in linen and carefully enclosed them in long jars which they capped securely. As it turned out, the members were so thoroughly scattered that they never returned to resume their common life, and the scrolls remained behind.

The 1951 excavation at Khirbet Qumran enlisted several Arabs as co-workers with the archeologists. Exchanging their shepherd staffs for the mattocks of the archeologist, the Arabs labored at removing the accumulated debris at Khirbet Qumran and searching for potsherds—the patient work of archeology. But when the season finished at the dig, their interest in these matters did not abate. They were now aware of the opportunities awaiting them in the Judean hills and were on the lookout for more caves. Thus a joint project of the Arab tribesmen and the trained archeologists began. The Arabs had the time, the patience, a minute knowledge of the terrain, and a desire for money; the archeologists had the desire for knowledge and the scientific know-how that could unearth the fragments, put them together, and reconstruct ancient history. It was no surprise to Father de Vaux that some Bedouin came to see him not long afterwards at the *École Biblique*. They had some new fragments for sale and claimed that they came from Cave 1. Father de Vaux was sceptical; perhaps the Arabs had found a new vein in the area. With no little humor and understanding of Bedouin ways, he cajoled them into admitting that the fragments came from a new source. He then allayed their fears and got them to agree to a full-fledged archeological dig under the protection of the police, their erstwhile enemies. Thus, at the beginning of 1952 began a six-week campaign in the caves of the Wadi Murabbaat, about ten miles southwest of Khirbet Qumran. It was soon discovered that this site gave evidence of occupation all the way back to the chalcolithic period (about 3500 B.C.) in Palestine. More important was the discovery of fragments of the most varied kind: Hebrew documents from the beginning of the Christian era (biblical books, such as Genesis, Exodus, Deuteronomy and Isaias); two letters signed by Simon ben Kosebah (seemingly the original name of Bar Kochba, the famed leader in the Second Jewish Revolt mentioned above). Apparently these caves had served as military outposts during the War of Bar Kochba and were captured about 135 A.D., by the Roman army. The most puzzling feature was that the finds of the Wadi Murabbaat seemed to have no connection with the Qumran community. Here is another cache of fragmentary ancient documents which call for an explanation. It seems that the rebels brought their treasured documents with them to the Wadi Murabbaat, one of their last refuges during the revolt.

But the tireless Bedouin kept bringing in new fragments which were supposed to come from the area of Cave 1. The archeologists organized a new campaign in March, 1952, and explored a five mile radius about Khirbet Qumran, investigating some forty caves. Again, several manuscript fragments of biblical and non-biblical works were found. In Cave 3 were discovered the famous copper scrolls, which were finally unrolled at Manchester, England, in January 1956; in June, it was announced that they contained a description of ancient treasures located in Palestine.

In the summer of this banner year of 1952, the Bedouin brought in new fragments from still a third source (after Qumran and the Wadi Murabbaat), the Wadi en-Nar, a continuation of the Kedron valley near the Mount of Olives which empties into the Dead Sea. This led to the Belgian excavation of Khirbet Mird in this area in 1953, with the first discovery of New Testament texts in the Dead Sea region; they were written in Greek and also in Syro-Palestinian, the language of the Christians of Palestine before the Islamic conquest in the seventh century.

The March, 1952, excavation had the most fruitful aftermath in September, 1952. The Bedouin had kept searching until they came upon the virtually inaccessible Cave 4, which yielded hundreds of fragments: over 300 different manuscripts (including Tobias in both Hebrew and Aramaic) are represented in this cache, all of them extremely fragmentary. Since this time fragments have been coming in to the authorities working in the Rockefeller Palestinian Museum in Arab Jerusalem. Money to buy these valuable pieces has been raised by the Jordan Government, various educational institutions, and the Vatican Library; it is believed that virtually all fragments outstanding had been acquired in 1956. The reader will recall from the Introduction that we do not yet know what yield will come from the latest discovery, Cave 11.

At Work on the Scrolls and Fragments

Preparation for publication is always an arduous, exacting task and archeologists are often guilty of extreme delays before final publication. But the scrolls experienced a better fate. Portions of Professor Sukenik's lot were published in 1948 and 1950 in his *Megilloth Genuzoth,* the "Geniza Scrolls," so-called because Sukenik mistakenly thought that the documents had been put in a geniza, a place for worn-out biblical texts, no longer fit for use. The complete publication appeared in 1954. The scrolls of the Syrian Archbishop were published by the American School of Oriental Research in 1950 (Isaias text and the Habacuc commentary) and 1951 (the Manual of Discipline).

But the publication of the thousands of fragments found in all the caves is an herculean task. The fragments of Cave 1 were completely published in 1955, but a reasonable estimate is that it will be about fifteen years before all the material from the other caves is published. The work involved is delicate and tedious: it is a battle of tweezers, brushes, and pen knives. The fragments, brittle and misshapen, are humidified in order to soften them and then flattened between plates. A camel-hair brush is used to clean them and the utmost care is required lest the ink come off with the small debris. Some fragments are too brittle for even this delicate treatment and must be supplied with a tape backing. Illegible fragments have to be treated with non-acid oil to bring out the letters. The greatest aid in rendering the letters legible has been infra-red photography.

After the fragments are cleansed and photographed, the process of identification begins. They are separated according to language (Hebrew,

Aramaic, etc.) and references to the Bible. Biblical fragments, identified by the use of lexicons, are separated from the non-biblical. This division must also be governed by the character of the letters, the quality of the leather, etc., so that fragments which originally belonged to one scroll can be kept together.

At the present time an international team of scholars is busily occupied with the fragments which are housed in the splendid Palestinian Museum. At the head is Father de Vaux. Three French priests, two Englishmen, two Americans, one German, and one Pole, also a priest, round out the team. The Americans are Professor Frank M. Cross, Jr., of Chicago, and Msgr. Patrick W. Skehan of the Catholic University of America. These scholars work secure in the knowledge that the scrolls and fragments are genuine. The very riches of the later discoveries have made impossible any doubt on this score. By 1956, discoveries were made in ten of the Qumran caves. During 1952–1955, six of these (Caves 3, 5, 7, 8, 9, 10) were discovered untouched by the archeologists. From 1947 to 1952, the other four were first discovered by the Bedouin, but were later subjected to complete investigation by competent archeologists. Of the ten, the yields in Cave 1 and Cave 4 are the greatest, and although the contents of

Cave 4 are only fragmentary, they are extremely important, as we shall see.

The Qumran Community

Who were the people who used the Qumran monastery and who possessed such an extensive library? Scholars had long known about the Essenes, a Jewish sect of the time of Christ, described in the works of Pliny, Philo, and Josephus. Comparisons were made between these ancient sources and the newly discovered scrolls and fragments. By and large, there are marked similarities. Both the Essenes and the Qumran community settled in the Judean wilderness near the Dead Sea, and Josephus adds that there were groups in every city. Both sources describe a Jewish group that lives a community life: common purse and common meals that are characterised by a great deal of protocol and by a priest's blessing. The general organization is also similar; there is a period of "postulancy" and "novitiate" before full membership described in both Josephus and the Qumran scrolls. There are other remarkable coincidences: an emphasis on seniority within the group; the necessity of majority consent to speak out of turn; even the detailed command that no spitting is allowed in the midst of the assembly. The Essenes and the Qumran community are both dedicated to the study and explanation of the Old Testament Torah, or Law. There is also a similarity of ritual and religious ideals: emphasis on discipline and asceticism, practices of ritual washings, etc. The majority of scholars today are agreed in recognizing the Qumran community as at least some form of Essenes. But there are still several unresolved discrepancies; for example, the ancient sources emphasize the peaceful habits of the Essenes, contrary to the newly found War scroll. The explanation may be that the accounts of Josephus and Philo are dated, that they describe a form of Essenism that developed out of the type we know from the scrolls. But the problem of identification with the Essenes is a relatively minor one; the important thing is that we have considerable knowledge about the Qumran community and their religious beliefs.

Although we do not have a clear picture of the origins of the Qumranites, it would seem that they are associated with the strong religious group of the *Hasidim*, or "the Pious" of Maccabean times (*circa* 165 B.C.; cf. 1 Mc. 2:42; 7:13). They looked on a certain person who is called the "teacher of righteousness" as their leader, if not their founder. He was persecuted by an unnamed enemy who is identified by many scholars as Alexander Jannaeus,

King and High Priest of the Jews (103–76 B.C.). The separatist tendency within the group is strikingly manifest in their retreat to the Judean desert away from their fellow Jews. But this withdrawal was prompted by more than mere separatism. They applied to themselves the text of Isaias 40:3, "in the wilderness prepare the way of the Lord." For them the preparation consisted in the study of the Law; they lived out their days at Qumran, praying and studying, interpreting the Scriptures and living in eager expectation for the coming of the Lord, when good would triumph over evil. This coming they called the "visitation of God," "the end-time," and they were living on its threshold.

They adopted a highly organized life of rigid discipline which is described in detail by the Manual of Discipline. The community was made up of priests, levites, and lay members, and the government was in the hands of a group of laymen and three priests. A superintendent presided over the members; his task was to examine and instruct the candidates during a rugged probationary period of two years. The ceremony of admission was called "entering the covenant." This was the "new covenant" predicted by the prophet Jeremias (31:31), because the community considered itself the true Israel. They still remained Jews and adhered to the principal Jewish doctrines, but they regarded their fellow Jews, who had not entered the new covenant, as children of darkness. Apparently they took no part in the Temple ritual in Jerusalem, although prayer played a large role in their life at Qumran. We shall see more detailed aspects of Qumran community life when we turn to the comparison with early Christianity in Chapter III.

The Contents of the Scrolls of Cave 1

Of the seven documents that make up the scrolls, two are copies of the Hebrew text of the book of Isaias. The rest are non-biblical works in various *genres:* paraphrase, commentary, rules, and psalms.

The Isaias scrolls and fragments. The complete text of Isaias is among the documents purchased by the Syrian Archbishop; it is a well-preserved scroll about twenty-four feet long and one foot wide. It had received much use and had been sewn several times where breaks had occurred. Our familiar division into chapters and verses, which dates from the medieval period, is naturally absent, but sectional divisions are indicated. In the margins and between the lines are found unknown signs as well as corrections. The second Isaias text, which Professor Sukenik originally purchased, is incomplete and often illegible except by infra-red photography. The last third of the book (38–66) is relatively complete and portions of earlier chapters, beginning with the tenth, are also present. Small pieces (varying from five to ten verses) of chapters 1–6 of the Sukenik manuscript were found on the floor of Cave 1 in the 1949 excavation. In addition, there is the unpublished yield from Cave 4: three scrolls with fragments from all parts of the book; two scrolls with fragments from early chapters (1–24; 1–14); a scroll with fragments of later chapters (28–50); and finally, a half dozen distinct fragments. The text of Isaias is also found explained or paraphrased in fragments coming from three different non-biblical compositions. The predilection of the community for this prophet is clearly manifest.

The Genesis Apocryphon. It will be recalled that this scroll was originally purchased by the Syrian Archbishop. It was at first thought that it might be the lost "Book of Lamech," because a detached piece of the scroll mentioned Lamech and his wife. For various reasons it was not unrolled until 1955; preliminary studies made by Jewish scholars of the Hebrew University indicate that it contains several stories about the Hebrew

Qumran Cave 1. Original opening is small black spot at top center.

(Photograph courtesy F. M. Cross, Jr.)

(Photograph courtesy F. M. Cross, Jr.)

Arrows point to the apertures of the virtually inaccessible Cave 4.

patriarchs written in Aramaic. The scroll measured about nine feet originally, although the beginning and end are now missing. Of the original eighteen columns, only three (containing Genesis 12–14) are complete, but there are considerable parts of six other pages. The author based his story on the Genesis narrative, but added many details and legends, such as the description of Sarah's beauty in Genesis 12.

The Habacuc Commentary. A relatively complete scroll (beginning at Hb. 1:2), this measures about five feet in length; it was about seven inches wide before the lower edge was eaten away. As its name indicates, it is a verse-by-verse interpretation of the book of Habacuc. The commentary is unique in that everything is explained with reference to the history of the group to which the commentator belongs. Habacuc's words are considered to be a prophecy of the historical events of the commentator's period, but it is exceedingly difficult to determine the historical allusions. With disturbing vagueness, the commentator refers to the Kittim, the house of Absalom, the wicked priest, the teacher of righteousness and other *dramatis personae*, without identifying them. Modern scholars have advanced several theories as to the identity of these persons, but there is as yet no common agreement; the most famous debate centers on the relationship of the teacher of righteousness to Jesus, as we shall see in Chapter III.

The Manual of Discipline. Another title is the *Serek Hayyahad,* or the "Order of the Community." It is a scroll about six feet (originally probably seven feet) long, and about nine inches wide. To this must now be added the two columns that were found in Cave 1 and published in 1955. The document begins with a remarkable statement of the lofty religious ideals of the community:

> to seek God . . . to do what is good and right before Him, as He commanded through Moses and all his servants, the prophets; to love all that He has chosen and hate all that He has rejected; to stay far from any evil and cling to every good deed; to carry out truth and justice and right in the land, and no longer to walk with a guilty, obstinate heart and lustful eyes, committing every evil; to bring into the covenant of love all those who dedicate themselves to carry out the precepts of God; and to be united in the congregation of God and walk perfect before Him . . . (1:1–8)

The rest of the scroll contains ceremonial directions for the annual observance of "entering the covenant," rules for organization and discipline, and the important description of the spirit of light and the spirit of darkness, and their "ways." At the end is a hymn, spoken in the first person and reminiscent of the scroll of Thanksgiving Psalms.

The War Scroll. The full title given by Professor Sukenik is "the War between the Children of Light and the Children of Darkness." It is nine feet long and contains nineteen columns, but the bottom third of each column has been worn away. The text gives the rules for conducting a holy war: the sons of Light (tribes of Levi, Juda and Benjamin) are arrayed against the sons of Darkness (Edomites, Moabites, Philistines, Greeks). God and His angels assist the army of Israelites, while Belial and his minions aid those on the side of darkness. In an apocalyptic war which seems to occur at the end of time, each opponent prevails three times, but in the seventh fray, the sons of Light are victorious.

The Thanksgiving Psalms. This title comes from the first lines of several of the psalms: "I give you thanks, O Lord." They are about thirty-five in number and closely resemble the Old Testament psalms in style and terminology. It is difficult to determine the background and circumstances of these psalms. Several describe the dire straits of the persecuted psalmist and commemorate God's intervention in his favor. Many scholars think that the teacher of righteousness may have been the author of some of them.

The Damascus Document. This work does not belong to the newly discovered scrolls, but fragments of it were discovered in Cave 6. It was originally discovered in the geniza (storeroom) of the Karaite synagogue in old Cairo in 1896, and was published shortly afterwards. Because it mentions an emigration to Damascus, the work received its name. But it is also referred to by another title, "the Sadokite Fragments," because of the sons of Sadok who figure so prominently in it. Experts differed greatly about this puzzling discovery, and the suggested dates ranged from the third century B.C., to the eleventh century A.D. With the publication of the Dead Sea scrolls, scholars immediately noticed their close relationship to the enigmatic Damascus Document. For example, the important figures of the Habacuc Commentary, the man of the lie and the teacher of righteousness, appear also in the Damascus Document. The terminology of these writings is remarkably the same: "the new covenant," "Belial," etc. The Damascus Document refers to the mysterious book of HGY which is likewise mentioned in the two columns belonging to the Manual of Discipline. A theory suggested by Father de Vaux is that the Damascus Document is the writing of those followers of the teacher of righteousness who fled to Damascus with their leader at the time that the Qumran monastery was abandoned (about 31 B.C.). It remains for future study to determine the precise relationship of this Damascus Document to the community.

These are the only complete works of the Qumran community which we possess, but it is important to emphasize that these are but a small portion of their library. The contents of the caves show that several of the so-called apocryphal books of this period were held in some honor by the people of Qumran: the Book of Enoch, Jubilees, the Testament of Levi, and others. In addition, there are entirely new works, the existence of which was unknown to us until the discoveries in the caves. Fragments of these writings have already been published, such as the Sayings of Moses, the Book of Mysteries, etc. The literary interests of the community were very wide; the newly discovered scrolls were far from being the sole inspiration of this people.

As yet, it is not clear how many of the scrolls and apocryphal works originated with the community itself. Certainly the Habacuc Commentary, the Manual of Discipline, the War Scroll, and the Thanksgiving Psalms seem to have been composed by a member of the sect, but much more study is necessary before any verdict can be given about the authorship of the rest, especially the apocrypha. As far as the biblical texts are concerned, it seems reasonable to presume that they were copied by members of the community, although some copies may date from a period before the community was formed. On the basis of the number and nature of the fragments, it seems that the most popular books of the Old Testament were the Pentateuch (especially Deuteronomy), the Psalms, Isaias, and Daniel. Every book in the traditional Hebrew Bible is represented among the fragments, except the book of Esther.

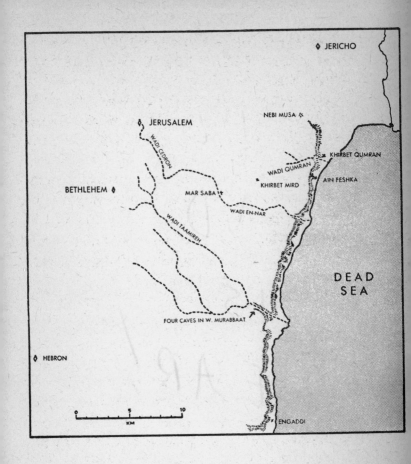

JERICHO

NEBI MUSA

JERUSALEM

WADI CEDRON

KHIRBET QUMRAN

WADI QUMRAN

BETHLEHEM

MAR SABA

KHIRBET MIRD

AIN FESHKA

WADI EN-NAR

WADI TAAMIREH

DEAD
SEA

FOUR CAVES IN W. MURABBAAT

HEBRON

0   5   10
        KM

ENGADDI

Chapter 2

THE
END
IS
NEAR!

The Old Testament in the Light of the Scrolls and Fragments

Where Does the Old Testament Come from?

Shortly after the appearance of the (Protestant) Revised Standard Version of the Old Testament in 1952, a storm of protest arose in various parts of the United States. Traditional phrases, to which people had been accustomed from their youth, had disappeared. For some, the translation was objectionable on theological grounds; for others, because of literary considerations. Catholics, too, have noticed a difference in their various translations of the Old Testament. All religious groups have become more conscious of the question: where does the English Bible come from?

For years the traditional English Catholic Bible has been the Douay-Rheims version, named after the French towns in which the translation was published: the New Testament, in 1582 and the Old in 1609–10. This version was made from the Latin, not from the original languages. The text used by the translators (exiled English priests), was the famous Latin Vulgate which St. Jerome had made from the original languages about 400 A.D. His Bible became the Bible of European Christendom until the Renaissance brought to modern man an interest in the ancient languages. It represents a substantially correct version of the Bible and is accurate in matters of faith and morals, but is not free of some errors in translation. Perhaps the last English translation of the Vulgate that will ever be made is the recent one by Monsignor Ronald Knox. Because the *Divino Afflante Spiritu* encyclical (1943) of Pope Pius XII gave such pronounced encouragement to translation from the original languages, Catholic scholars of the United States began a new version, called the Confraternity of Christian Doctrine translation. Volumes I (Genesis to Ruth) and III (Sapiential Books) have been published thus far.

It is evident from this that English translations of the Old Testament go back to the original languages, either directly, or through the Latin, as in the case of the Douay-Rheims version. Since the Old Testament was written originally in Hebrew for the most part, the history of the Hebrew text is very important. How can we be sure that the standard Hebrew text represents the original work which, for example, Isaias or Jeremias wrote? Do we have any history of the

Hebrew text, by which we are able to determine what it was like in the seventeenth century, or in the fifth century, or at the time of Christ, or even before?

As we might expect, the history of the Hebrew Bible becomes cloudier the farther back we go. Since the invention of printing in the fifteenth century, practically all printed Hebrew Bibles are the same. Before that, in the days when books were copied by hand, there is more variation between copies, due to human errors in the exacting work of writing out lengthy manuscripts. On the whole, however, the scribes were extremely careful, and there is no substantial variation in these manuscripts, of which the earliest dated is the *Codex Petropolitanus* (916 A.D.), preserved in Moscow. The reason for this striking uniformity is the work of the Masoretes, Jewish scribes who studied and transmitted the Hebrew text from the sixth to about the eleventh centuries, and who have given their name to the standard Masoretic text of the Old Testament. Up to their time Hebrew was written without vowels; in order to ensure a definite reading and eliminate all ambiguity, they devised a system of vowel signs and punctuation which rendered the Hebrew text practically immutable.

The next important evidence in tracing the history of the Hebrew Bible is the Latin Vulgate translation by St. Jerome about 400 A.D. When we examine his work, we discover that while it agrees substantially with our present Hebrew Bible, there are differences in several passages. This means that the Hebrew text he was translating differed, even if only slightly, from the later text established by the Jewish Masoretes. There is a Jewish tradition that about 100 A.D. one form of the text was chosen as official and all the others were destroyed. This would account for the relatively complete agreement between the Hebrew text used by St. Jerome and that used by the Masoretes.

The Greek translation (called the Septuagint) that was made in the second century B.C. is a very important witness to the state of the Hebrew text because it gets behind the "official" form of the Masoretic text of the Old Testament. For example, the book of Jeremias is about one-eighth shorter in the Greek and follows a different arrangement of chapters. The Septuagint translation, although produced originally by Jews, became the official Old Testament for the early Church; in reaction, the Greek-speaking Jews produced new translations in the second century: those of Aquila, Symmachus, and Theodotion. Thus, in the course of time, the Greek Old Testament assumed so many various forms that Origen in the third century attempted to establish one form. His effort was the monumental work, the *Hexapla,* which contained in six columns the Hebrew text along with various forms of the Greek text current in his day. Only a few fragments of Origen's work have survived.

Thus far we have traced briefly the genealogy of the modern Hebrew Bible back to about 200 B.C. We might compare the history of the Hebrew Old Testament to the hypothetical experience of a rigger climbing a pole: the first part of his ascent is all the same; he jams his spikes into the wood and ascends. But as he nears the top, his spikes find the wood slightly different. Similarly, as we go back through the history of the Bible, spikes can be driven into the long transmission of the Hebrew text. St. Jerome's Latin translation is one such approach, giving us a picture of the Hebrew text about 400 A.D. The Septuagint translation is another, telling us the state of the Hebrew text in the second century B.C. Now with the Qumran discoveries there is another spike that can be driven in. The great gap that existed in the evidence between the Septuagint and the Vulgate is being closed, thanks to the various scrolls and fragments. Instead of trying to determine the form of the Hebrew text through translations (Latin and Greek), we now have several copies of the text itself. Instead of working with a Hebrew text that has been standardized in spelling, pronunciation, and even in its reading by the traditions of the Masoretes, we have reached far behind them to copies that were made five or six centuries before the Masoretes lived. For some books at least (Ecclesiastes and Daniel), we now have copies that were made less than two hundred years after the books were first written. This advantageous situation was never even dreamt of before 1947. The only ancient Hebrew text in a continuous piece was the fragment called the Nash papyrus, containing merely the Decalogue, which has been dated to the second or early first century B.C. Now however, scholars have been introduced to the "pre-history" of the Masoretic text and they hope to fix more securely the original readings of many uncertain passages by the use of textual criticism.

Textual Criticism

Textual criticism is an art that is practiced in all fields of literature. Its goal is to discover the form of a text as it was written by the original author. Thus, in English literature, scholars have determined as closely as possible the original words written by Shakespeare in his plays. They have compared early editions (quartos and folios) in order to establish the correct reading. For example, Hamlet's soliloquy in Act I, Scene II, begins "O that this too too solid flesh would melt, thaw and resolve itself into a dew!" A significant variant, preferred by some, is "sullied" flesh. However, the weight of the evidence is in favor of "solid" flesh. Similarly, biblical scholars must sift all the evidence in order to determine the correct reading of the Bible.

Manuscripts and copies are called "external evidence" for the text; they are objective evidence in support of a reading. In some cases, especially when there is no satisfactory objective evidence, one is forced to use "internal evidence,"—that given by the context or sense of a passage. Thus, when a word or phrase clearly does not suit the context or has the appearance of being a later insertion or explanatory gloss, the textual critic feels authorized to make a change in the text. His purpose is to correct a clearly unsatisfactory reading that could hardly have come from the original author. But since he has no concrete evidence (such as manuscripts) in favor of his change, he has to resort to reasons internal to the book (context, etc.) to justify his change. Such internal evidence is in reality a well-educated guess. But it may often yield the original reading.

In the case of the Bible, the textual critic uses both kinds of evidence. For the Old Testament the mass of external evidence is incredibly large. We have not only the thousands of hand-copies of the Hebrew Bible that have been preserved, but also the several old translations besides the Septuagint and the Vulgate described above. There are the translation of the Old Testament into Syriac (called the "Peshitto," dating from about 200 A.D.) and the paraphrases in the Aramaic language (called the "Targum," first written down in the second century A.D.). The magnitude of the external evidence available for textual criticism of the Old Testament far exceeds that for any profane book that has been written in antiquity. It is the work of the scholar to weigh this evidence and by means of it to establish a "critical text" of the Bible, one which represents as nearly as possible the exact words which the author originally wrote.

For an example of a "critical text," we may turn to the new Confraternity of Christian Doctrine translation which we have already mentioned. In the original edition, published by the St. Anthony Guild Press, there is an appendix which contains the textual notes. Although intended only for specialists, these notes are important because they indicate the care which went into the work of translation. The scholars used the traditional Hebrew text as the basis of their work. But they did not translate blindly; they compared the Hebrew with the ancient versions, such as the Septuagint and Vulgate, in order to correct the mistakes which have crept into the Hebrew text in the course of time. Each departure from the Hebrew text is noted and the basis for the departure is given: the Septuagint, or some other version, or perhaps plain conjecture, when no evidence is available from any version or Hebrew manuscript. The first example given in the appendix is concerned with the phrase "and so it was," which runs like a refrain throughout the first chapter of Genesis. The textual note tells us that this phrase is to be read in verse 6 instead of verse 7. The evidence is that the Septuagint read it that way, and also such a reading agrees with the general style of the first chapter which elsewhere (in verses 9, 11, etc.) always locates this phrase after God's command ("Let there be . . ."). It is up to the judgment and experience of the scholars to determine in such cases what the original text must have been.

It may be thought that in the case of the Bible there is no need for textual investigations, that

God would not allow textual errors to creep into it during the years it has been handed down. But that is simply not true. God did not choose to exercise such a miraculous Providence over the books of the Bible. It is true that we can be certain that God's message has been preserved, that we have substantially intact the works that the authors first wrote; but in very many instances we are ignorant of the exact words and phrases, and even of the meaning. Therefore, textual criticism is necessary and important. In this connection we must bear in mind the admonition of Pope Pius XII in his encyclical, *Divino Afflante Spiritu:*

In the present day indeed this art, which is called textual criticism and which is used with great and praiseworthy results in the editions of profane writings, is also quite rightly employed in the case of the Sacred Books, because of that very reverence which is due to the Divine Oracles. For its very purpose is to insure that the sacred text be restored, as perfectly as possible, be purified from the corruptions due to the carelessness of the copyists and be freed, as far as may be done, from glosses and omissions, from the interchange and repetition of words and from all other kinds of mistakes, which are wont to make their way gradually into writings handed down through many centuries.

The New Finds and the Text of the Hebrew Bible

We are now at a point where we may ask: what value are the scrolls and fragments for the text of the Hebrew Bible? The following conclusions can be formulated in answer:

1. We have another window through which to view the Hebrew text at a relatively young period of its life—in the era before Christ. The new discoveries teach us that the form of the traditional Masoretic text goes back further than we realized —to the second century B.C.

2. There is striking proof, if proof was ever needed, that our traditional text of the Old Testament has not been seriously corrupted in the process of its long transmission. The most noteworthy example of agreement with the current Hebrew text is to be found in the two Isaias scrolls of Cave 1. These are about a thousand years older than the oldest Hebrew copy of Isaias that we have, yet there are few real differences from the traditional text. We now appreciate the painstaking care with which such a text has been transmitted. As indicated in Chapter 1, there are also

fragments of about eight distinct copies of Isaias, most of which were found in Cave 4. Until they are all published, it will be impossible to judge the results. However, it is more or less expected that they will, in large measure, reflect the same form of text as the scrolls. The correspondence of the Qumran texts to the medieval Masoretic Old Testament can be exemplified in several other cases besides Isaias. Some of the most interesting fragments are those of Leviticus from Cave 1. These are written in the old Hebrew script which was current before the square script that is familiar to us today, and are dated by some to about the fourth century B.C.; yet they agree almost entirely with the Masoretic text.

3. We have greater evidence of a certain fluidity in the Hebrew text in the period before Christ; no uniform text was accepted by all the Jewish communities. This fact was not unknown to scholars before 1947, but it was reached by inference from the Septuagint translation. There was no evidence in Hebrew itself until the discoveries at Qumran. Many scholars had pointed out the significant differences from the Masoretic text, which were to be seen in the arrangement and reading of the ancient Greek translation. Sometimes it is obvious that the reason for the differences was that the Hebrew underlying the Greek differed from

our present Hebrew text. But in many instances, one could not be sure; perhaps the translator had made a mistake, or just freely paraphrased what we have in our present text. Thus, many scholars considered that the Greek translation had more value for the history of interpretation than for textual criticism. It is just at this point that the new fragments, especially those of Cave 4, enter the picture. Many of them present a text which is the same as the Hebrew from which the Septuagint was made.

We can turn to Deuteronomy 32:8 for an example. In the new Catholic Confraternity translation, the phrase "sons of God" is found in this verse and the textual notes declare that this is done on the basis of the Septuagint against the Masoretic text which reads "sons of Israel." Now in a tiny Qumran fragment is found the first evidence in any ancient Hebrew manuscript for "sons of God" in Deuteronomy 32:8. We can summarize our evidence:

"Sons of Israel"—traditional Masoretic text.
"Sons of God"—Septuagint *and* Qumran fragment.

It is easy to understand why "sons of Israel" came to be substituted in the traditional Hebrew text for "sons of God." The sons of God are the supernal beings of God's heavenly court; these guard all the nations except Israel which is protected directly by the Lord. Since there was danger that in the polytheistic environment in which Judaism found itself, these beings might be adored (see Deuteronomy 4:19–20; 29:24–25), some scribe judged that a change of text was in order. He eliminated "sons of God," for "sons of Israel," who were clearly mortal men. But we may now be sure that "sons of God" is the correct and original reading, and that it was in the Hebrew text underlying the Septuagint translation.

Summing up, we may say that we have now three lines going back to the early pre-Christian form of the Hebrew text: 1) the Masoretic text, now shown to go back to the second century B.C.; 2) the Greek translation, put in a new light by the fragments; 3) the Qumran texts themselves, which go back before the time of the Masoretes and reveal a relative fluidity in the readings of the Hebrew text.

4. We may reasonably expect that some original readings will be recovered with the help of the scrolls and fragments. This would seem to be the case for 1 Samuel 23:10–12 and, with perhaps less probability, for 1 Samuel 1:22, according to the

evidence of some extremely important fragments from Cave 4. These fragments belonged originally to two manuscripts of the Books of 1 and 2 Samuel (according to the Vulgate, 1 and 2 Kings). Manuscript 4QSam^a (i.e., manuscript 1 of Samuel from Cave 4 at Qumran) has grown considerably since the initial discovery, due to later purchases from the Bedouin. It now shows portions of 23 (out of an original 33) columns making up 1 Samuel, and also portions of 24 (originally 24 also) columns of 2 Samuel. These fragments date from the first century B.C. The second manuscript, called 4QSam^b, is extremely fragmentary; it has the same form of text as 4QSam^a, although it is earlier by perhaps a hundred years.

When portions of 4QSam^a were first published in 1953, they attracted considerable attention because of the addition in 1 Samuel 1:22: "and I will present him as a Nazarite." This clause, which may very well be original, seems to have been lost in the traditional Hebrew text by the common error of *homoioteleuton:* the copyist's eye went from the word "forever," which occurs just before the clause, to the second "forever," which follows immediately upon the clause. It had always been assumed on the basis of 1 Samuel 1:11, that Samuel was a Nazirite (fulfilling the conditions of Numbers 6:1–21), but now there is the explicit statement found in the Qumran fragments.

The second manuscript of Samuel (4QSam^b) has preserved the original reading in 1 Samuel 23:10–12. When the entire passage is reconstructed with the help of the fragments, it runs thus:

10. Then David said, "O Lord God of Israel, your servant has heard for certain that Saul seeks to enter Ceila to destroy the city on account of me. 11. But now, will Saul go down, as your servant has heard? O Lord God of Israel, tell your servant." And the Lord said, "He will go down." 12. Then David asked, "Will the men of Ceila hand me and my men over to Saul?" "They will," replied the Lord.

If these verses are compared with the Hebrew or with the traditional Douay-Rheims translation from St. Jerome's Vulgate, it will be seen that David's question about the men of Ceila is mistakenly repeated in verse 11, having gotten in there from verse 12, where it belongs. On the other hand, the Greek Septuagint translation omits the Lord's answer to David's first question, and also the second question, so that to David's question about Saul, the Lord answers, rather cryptically, "they will deliver." There can hardly be any doubt that the Qumran fragments have preserved the correct reading.

5. The Qumran texts also tell us something about the early editing of the Hebrew books. Some of the older books, such as Isaias, appear to have been prepared or edited in Babylonia and taken back by the Jewish exiles when they returned to Palestine in the sixth and fifth centuries B.C. The proof of this is to be gathered from the complete Isaias scroll of Cave 1. Here the foreign names of the Babylonian officers are spelled according to the correct Babylonian manner, as "Sharusur" for "Shareser," and "Turtan" for "Tartan" (Is. 37:38; 20:1). This Babylonian spelling has been completely forgotten and distorted in the later and artificial Hebrew spelling of the Masoretes, which was the only one known to us. The best explanation of the Babylonian spelling is that the text was edited in Babylon.

6. We are acquiring a more detailed knowledge of the origins of the Greek Septuagint translation, which was made originally in Egypt. For certain books, such as Genesis and Kings, it appears that the Hebrew text underlying the Greek translation had been transmitted for some time among the Jews living in Egypt; again, the evidence is from certain proper names which have been "Egyptianized" before entering the Greek translation.

In connection with the Septuagint, a new find which does not belong to Qumran possessions should be mentioned. In late August, 1952, the Taamireh Bedouin discovered in an unidentified cave, apparently in the Wadi en-Nar, important fragments of a parchment scroll which had been abandoned about 135 A.D. The manuscript, which contains extensive parts of the Greek text of the Minor Prophets, gives evidence of much use, so the end of the first century A.D. is a likely date for its composition. Preliminary study of this text has indicated that it is an "improved" text, or recension, which had been worked over by Jewish scholars. This is surprising since it has been widely held that the prestige of the Septuagint among the Christians had brought it into disfavor with the Jews. Moreover, the similarities between this new find and the extant parts of Aquila's second century translation show that Aquila did not make a new translation; he used this form of the Greek Septuagint as a basis for his own work. Another problem that seems to be solved by this discovery is the biblical quotations of St. Justin. The celebrated apologist, in his arguments with Jewish opponents, notably Trypho, quoted the Septuagint in the form that they used, accusing them of falsifying the prophecies. But apart from St. Justin there was never any evidence for the kind of biblical text that he quotes, and the world of scholarship generally repudiated his quotations. Now we see that Justin's biblical quotations agree with the text of the newly discovered manuscript.

7. The late dates given to several of the books of the Bible by some scholars will have to be revised. Cave 4 yielded four fragments of a manuscript of Ecclesiastes which were published in 1954. On the basis of paleography these are to be dated at about 150 B.C., and a third century date for the actual composition of the book is likely. The theories which placed the date of the original composition after 150 B.C. are proved wrong. There has been a trend away from dating any of the Psalms in the period of the Maccabees (second century, B.C.) and this trend is further reinforced by the evidence of the scrolls. The Thanksgiving Psalms belonging to the Qumran community suggest, by their style and content, that they were written long after the canonical Psalms of the Old Testament. Besides, the discovery of fragments of commentaries on certain Psalms indicates that the collections which make up the Psalter had already been finished by the time of the Qumran community.

8. The last books of the Old Testament, such as Sirach, Daniel and Wisdom, were composed about the time that the Qumran community was in exist-

ence. It is possible therefore, that the new discoveries will throw some light on these books.

Sirach (Ecclesiasticus) was written originally in Hebrew about 190 B.C., and translated into Greek fifty years later by the author's grandson. The Hebrew text was lost for centuries, but in 1896 extensive fragments were found in the Jewish synagogue at Cairo and two fragments of Sirach have been discovered in Cave 2 at Qumran. There is a marked similarity in grammar and linguistic peculiarities between the Hebrew Sirach and the scrolls. But in content there is hardly any similarity; the closest parallel is a passage in Sirach 33 that resembles the dualistic doctrine of the Manual of Discipline (3:13–4:26). At Sirach 51:12 is a litany of sixteen verses which is found in the Hebrew text but not in the Greek and other versions. Because of the reference to the sons of Sadok in this litany, it has been thought to have originated with the "Sadokites," as the people of Qumran called themselves. The litany can be read in the footnote to the new Catholic Confraternity translation of the Sapiential Books.

Among the fragments from Cave 4 has been found a story concerning Nabonidus of Babylon that is important for judging the literary genre of the book of Daniel. It had already been known that Nabonidus was the last king of the neo-

Babylonian dynasty (555–539 B.C.). His reign was largely spent between the oasis of Tema in the Arabian desert (for seven years) and Babylon, his capital. His residence at Tema is an unusual departure from the practice of his predecessors, which the new fragments apparently attempt to explain. They contain his prayer at the time he was afflicted with a dread disease (*šhn'*), (the same word describes Job's disease in Job 2:4), for seven years. God sends him a Jewish diviner who orders Nabonidus to worship the most High God (Yahweh). Then there follows a portion of a letter from the Jewish diviner who seems to imply that false idols cannot grant the health which Yahweh alone can give.

This story belongs to the literary *genre* of *haggadah* which is represented in other Jewish writings of the period (e.g., the story of Susanna). In this literary form an historical person is the subject of a "story" that is not historical. The story is freely developed for the purpose of religious edification. Thus we have an example of the ends to which a Jewish writer might turn a few facts. Is this type of writing to be excluded from the Bible? By no means. It may even be that the writer of the book of Daniel has followed the same literary device. There is a strong resemblance between the story in the fragments and in Daniel

3:31–4:34. In the biblical narrative the king is Nabuchodonosor and the wise Jew is Daniel, who alone can tell and interpret the king's dream. Daniel foretells seven years of insanity and the king is afflicted. Thus, in both stories there is a Babylonian king who is struck with a seven-year disease and in both the purpose is the same: to glorify Yahweh and to underline the nothingness of idols.

It would seem that a popular tradition concerning Nabonidus was circulating at the time of the author of the book of Daniel. He took this tradition and applied it for his own purposes to king Nabuchodonosor, who is the central royal figure in Daniel, cc. 1–4. We cannot determine whether this was an oral or written tradition that the biblical author used, but it is hard to escape the conclusion that he *is* using this same tradition to make a point in his religious message.

The book of Wisdom was written in the first century B.C., by a Jew of Alexandria, in Egypt. Scholars have long argued the measure of influence which the Greek world exercised upon the author, especially as regards the doctrine of immortality which is expressed in it. Now some scholars have indicated several parallels between Wisdom and the Manual of Discipline which would indicate that the development of the doctrine of a blessed immortality is to be explained from within Judaism itself, rather than from any outside influence.

New Vistas on the Hebrew and Aramaic Languages

The greatest importance attaches to the scrolls and fragments because they illustrate the history of the Hebrew Bible; by the same token they enrich our knowledge of the Hebrew language itself and its sister-language, Aramaic.

1. Every language grows and develops. We are all conscious of the difference between the English language as Chaucer wrote it and that same language as written by T. S. Eliot. The spelling, the rules of grammar, even the style of writing—all these are affected by the passage of years. The more literary evidence we can gather from the literature before and after Chaucer's period, the more exactly we can chart the course of development. Fortunately, there is a relatively large amount of English literary works that can be called upon for comparison. As regards Hebrew, however, there is a dearth of material in the period just before and just after Christ, and it is precisely from this era that the scrolls and fragments date. By studying the new material from a linguistic point of view, scholars will be able to achieve great

advances in our knowledge of Hebrew grammar. This benefit from the scrolls is the least sensational of all, but it is nonetheless important.

2. It has been almost an axiom in biblical history to say that Hebrew was a "dead" language in the two centuries just before the Christian era. To a certain extent this is true; we know that Aramaic was carried through the Near East by the Persian Empire (sixth to fourth centuries), to be followed by Greek after Alexander's conquest (about 300 B.C.). We know also that in this period the Jewish Targums began; these were paraphrases of the Hebrew Bible in Aramaic for the sake of those who no longer knew Hebrew. But the scholarly world was unprepared for the extensive body of literature in Hebrew which belonged to the Qumran community. It is written in biblical Hebrew, which, although not the classical language of the earlier books, is still very much alive. Since the code of life for the Qumran community was drawn up in this language, it is to be presumed that it was read and understood by all the members.

3. During the first half of the twentieth century, considerable debate raged over the question of the Aramaic sources of the New Testament; some scholars held that the Gospels were written originally in this language. One argument that was urged against them was the absence of a body of Aramaic

(Photograph courtesy F. M. Cross, Jr.)

The room above that in the foreground contained the writing benches of the community. No doubt some of the MSS. were prepared in the community scriptorium. (Kh. Qumran, looking south).

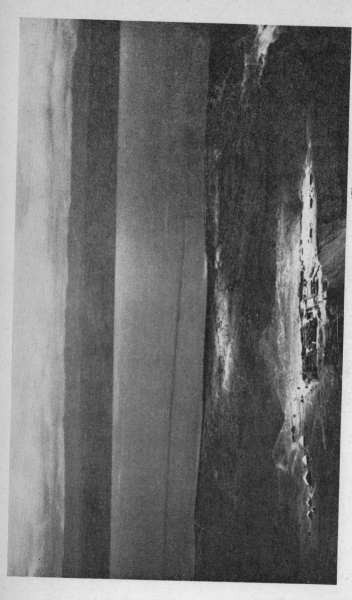

Air view of Qumran (in foreground) showing Dead Sea and hills of Moab in the background.

(Photograph courtesy Abbé Jean Starcky)

literature dating from the time of Christ; the only evidence came from inscriptions. It would seem that this argument, an argument *ex silentio,* can no longer stand. The evidence of the Qumran fragments points to a sizable amount of literature in Aramaic; over sixty different Aramaic manuscripts have been noted, and among these the books of Tobias (Tobit) and the apocrypal Testament of Levi have been identified. This does not mean that we have evidence that the Gospels were written in Aramaic; it means that we have evidence of a body of Aramaic literature existing at the time the Gospels were being written. This increases the probability that at least parts of the Gospels were written originally in Aramaic. It will be the task of future studies, after a comparison with the newly discovered Qumran literature, to determine to what extent an Aramaic text underlies our Greek Gospels.

In recent years a hue and cry has been raised over the "language which Jesus spoke." It is generally agreed that Aramaic was the native tongue He would have learned as a youth. The great difficulty which prevented scholars from identifying the language more exactly has been the fact that we have no literary works which date from both the age and the area in which Jesus lived. The reader may ask if this problem will be solved by the Aramaic writings which have been found among the scrolls and fragments. Since so little of this Aramaic material has been published thus far, it is too early to give more than a tentative answer. But it does appear that these Jewish Palestinian Aramaic writings from Qumran should exemplify the language of Jesus. Being literary documents, they will not reflect the ordinary spoken language, and therefore they will be somewhat remote from the Gospel dialogue. In every language, the written style differs from the spoken style, and there were differences in the spoken language of Jesus' day, as proved by Peter's manner of speech which betrayed his Galilean origin. But even when we allow for this, it would still appear true that these fragments contain the native language of Jesus: the Palestinian Aramaic of his day.

Chapter 3

The New Testament in the Light
of the Scrolls and Fragments

Introduction

We have seen that the relevance of the new discoveries to the Old Testament is primarily in the realm of textual criticism: by illuminating the early history of the Hebrew Bible, the Qumran manuscripts help us determine more accurately the original words of the Old Testament. On the other hand, their value for New Testament studies lies in the realm of interpretation, for they shed new light on the historical and religious background of the New Testament. Only a few books of the New Testament, written in Greek and Syro-Palestinian, were among the fragments found at Khirbet Mird in 1953, and they will be of some importance for the history of the text of the New Testament. But the real contribution to New Testament studies comes from the scrolls and fragments of the works written by the Qumran community, such as the Manual of Discipline. This non-biblical literature, along with the apocrypha and the works of Josephus and a few others, are our primary sources for the history of the so-called inter-Testamental period, i.e., between the time that the Old Testament came to an end and the New Testament began. Because the new finds throw light on the language and world of ideas in the New Testament, there is a foundation for the statement of some scholars about the "revolution" they have caused. But the scrolls have not revolutionized New Testament *theology*; rather, they have filled in an almost unknown background to the historical origins of Christianity.

The relation of early Christianity to its background is not a new problem. While recognizing the general antecedents of Christianity in the Old Testament, scholars have attempted to determine the specific influences upon Jesus and the New Testament writers. For example, how closely does the teaching of Jesus resemble the teaching of the Pharisees, the most powerful Jewish group of His day, and about whom we are best informed? Two German scholars, Strack and Billerbeck, have published several volumes illustrating New Testament doctrines from the Jewish sources, the Talmud and Midrash. On the other hand, many studies have been made of the Greek influence upon Christianity, particularly as shown in St. Paul, who was so very much a man of the world. Some may think that this type of study is "dangerous" for Christianity, or that at best it is unimportant because it concerns secondary features in the Christian religion. Both views are mistaken. Far from being "dangerous," renewed study of the religious background from which the Church emerged highlights the unique revelation which Christ brought to the world. This alone would make such study important. But there is another reason: this study teaches us something of the way in which God has given His revelation. He did not treat the world as a *tabula rasa,* which had nothing to offer to His message. To convey His revelation, He built upon "the elements of the world" (Col. 2:8), and especially upon the religion of the Old Testament. He had to speak the language of the men He would draw to Himself. It is true that there have been exaggerations in the studies concerning the origins of Christianity; too many glib assertions have been made about evolution and development. Parallel doctrines do not necessarily indicate an evolution from one religious movement into another; one must beware of oversimplification. Nor does the word "evolution" do justice to religious developments. Christianity, if you will, evolved from Israel of the Old Testament, but it is necessary to recall that this was not *merely* a natural, historical development.

Throughout this chapter, one must keep in mind that the teachings of the Qumran community and the New Testament both have their roots in the Jewish Old Testament. It is no surprise, therefore, to see similar phraseology in them. Both speak of spirit, flesh, conversion, holiness, sin, knowledge, secret, revelation, covenant, etc. Both mention the justice of God, the wrath of God, the holy spirit; each thought that it formed the new alliance or new covenant foretold by Jeremias (31:31). These and other similarities will appear as we consider the following themes: John the Baptist, the writings of St. John the Evangelist, the Sermon on the Mount, the Acts and Epistles, and finally, the alleged parallel between the teacher of righteousness and Jesus.

John the Baptist

The *Illustrated London News* for Sept. 3, 1955, published an excellent picture of the remains of the Qumran community building, along with the blithe assertion that John the Baptist "was almost certainly an Essene and must have studied and worked in this building: he undoubtedly derived the idea of ritual immersion, or baptism, from them." What evidence is there for this statement?

There are three general points under which we

may group the parallels between John the Baptist and the Qumranites. 1) Both have priestly origins. John was a priest, the son of Zachary who belonged to "the class of Abias" (Lk. 1:5), and he lived in a family that was intensely pious and impregnated with Messianism. The Qumran community was a priestly community, calling themselves the sons of Sadok (David's priest); "priestly" perfection was demanded of the members (1QS 8:4–10).

2) Both find their inspiration in Isaias 40:3: "In the wilderness prepare the way of the Lord; make straight in the desert a highway for our God." This was, as it were, the charter of the Qumran community (1QS 8:13–15; 9:19–20). By their study and prayer in common, apart from outsiders, they prepared in the Judean desert for the final period, the Messianic era. In a similar way, the Baptist identifies himself to the exasperated priests from Jerusalem who question him; he is the voice of one shouting in the wilderness, "Prepare the way of the Lord" (Jn. 1:23). The Messias is coming and a way must be prepared for him. Both John and the Qumranites are following the Messianic tradition of the Old Testament which describes Israel returning in a new "Exodus" to the desert to repent (cf. Os. 2:14ff.). But John's message is singularly free of the emphasis which Qumran attaches to observance of the Law: "Repent, for

the Kingdom of Heaven is at hand" (Mt. 3:2); he does not speak of a "way," but of repentance and a kingdom. For Qumran, mankind is divided into two irreconcilable groups: the sons of Light and the sons of Darkness, with no common ground between them. But the Baptist's message is directed to *all*, even to the Sadducees whom he invites to repent. Curiously enough, he calls the Sadducees a "brood of vipers" (Mt. 3:7). Similarly, the Qumranites applied to their enemies this phrase of Isaias (59:5), "viper's eggs" (DD 5:13–14), but without an appeal to change their ways. John's preaching carried him to both sides of the Jordan, to Ainon near Salem, "because there was much water there" (Jn. 3:23), and to Bethany, thirty miles to the south.

3) The rite of baptism at Qumran shows similarities to that of John. Several times in the New Testament, John is described as "baptizing." His baptism was one "of conversion unto the remission of sins" (Lk. 3:3), which is difficult to define. We do know that Jewish proselytes had a form of washing which indicated a sloughing off of the past when one became incorporated into Israel. But the origins and ramifications of the whole pre-Christian baptist movement are shrouded in mystery. At this point the Qumran material throws some light on John's baptism. We know that they

practiced baptism (1QS 3:4–9; 5:13–14), and it will be recalled that the Qumran excavations uncovered several cisterns and pools, one of them with fourteen steps leading down into it. It would appear that the Essenes practiced several washings, and that these were self-imposed, in contrast with the role of a baptizer in the rite of John. But the Qumran writings explicitly demand interior purification *before* undergoing the rite itself (1QS 3:6–11). In a similar way, John laid emphasis on a change of heart and corresponding conduct (Lk. 3:7–9). But they part company as far as the significance of the rite of washing was concerned. In line with Jewish thought, the Essenes conceived of the washing as a cleansing of the flesh which had been rendered impure; hence there were regulations prohibiting contact with those who did not belong to the community (1QS 5:14–20; 9:8–9). For John the exterior act of washing implies no preoccupation with such ritual purity; he never encourages separation from others. Rather, his baptism is a simple affirmation or symbol of the interior change of heart; that is why it was administered only once.

Qumran and the Baptist come together again in the doctrine of a second Baptism. John announced a baptism with the Holy Spirit and fire which one mightier than he was to administer (Lk. 3:16).

In Christian times, the Church condemned as heretical the sects which interpreted this fire in a literal sense. But what is the fire of which John speaks? It is rather unlikely that he would be foretelling the descent of the Holy Spirit upon the Apostles. It is the fire which is the customary accompaniment of the eschatological end-time, the Messianic period. Such judgment by fire is a prominent theme in the preaching of the prophets (Is. 10:16–19; 30:27–33; Am. 7:4, etc.). John envisions two baptisms, his own and a later one that will come in the final period; one complements the other. Similarly, the Essenes preach a second baptism. In a description of the eschatological period, when God will "visit" His people, the Manual of Discipline relates that God will "purify all the actions of men by His truth"; "by a holy spirit He will cleanse (man) from all wicked deeds and sprinkle him with a spirit of truth" (IQS 4:20–22); this will bring to man a "knowledge of the Most High," and the "wisdom of the sons of heaven." Here is a remarkable counterpart to John's baptism by the Holy Spirit. Both are eschatological; both are the work of the spirit of God. It seems as though the Precursor is pointing to the Sacramental Baptism established by Jesus, in terms of the Qumran expectations. In the Judean world in which John preached, his doctrine was surely familiar to his contemporaries, although it pointed to a fulfillment that was as yet vague.

It is too much to say that John "derived" his baptismal practice from the Essenes. The possibility also exists that both John and the Qumran community are reflections of a widespread baptist movement during this period, of which we know relatively little. His baptism is not part of a community ritual in a sect which encouraged *many* sacred lustrations. His is not repeated, but is merely an initiation into the repentance he called for. John is a prophet of doom, calling for conversion before the storm to come; he does not legislate for a community, as the teacher of righteousness does.

In favor of a Qumran training for the Baptist is the fact that he spent much of his life in the Judean desert (Mt. 3:1). It is most probable that he knew the community that had settled at Qumran and that he had to determine his own position with regard to them. To that extent, at least, he was influenced by them. No objection can be raised to his having been a member of the community. But the evidence we have reviewed is not strong enough to warrant the statement that he was a member. Some scholars have suggested that John, orphaned at the death of Zachary and Elizabeth, was "adopted" by the community, a practice which Josephus relates concerning the Essenes. But this is no more than a guess. All we can be sure of is that John lived in the Judean desert where Qumran is located; he must have had some contact with them because he echoes several points that are found in their teachings.

The Writings of St. John

Down to very recent times it has been fashionable to take for granted that the Gospel of St. John was written in the second century. One reason for this position is the alleged influence of gnostic ideas upon the Gospel. The Gnostics, heretics of the early Church who split into various sects during the second to the fourth centuries, laid emphasis on the knowledge (gnosis) of God who is Light and Life. This emphasis is also typical of St. John's writings. The author was not himself a Gnostic, scholars admitted, but he used gnostic terminology and ideas in combatting these heretics. Some scholars dissented from this verdict and now find their judgment confirmed by archeological discoveries. In the year before the scrolls came to light, there was an important discovery at Chenoboskion in Upper Egypt: a batch of about forty gnostic treatises, written in Coptic and dating from the third and fourth centuries, A.D. The gradual publication and study of these works reveal that it is an utter mistake to consider the Gospel as a product of a gnostic *milieu;* they show that this heretical doctrine is definitely later than the Gospel, although the early Gnostics used this Gospel in their teaching. At the same time, the scrolls have shed light on the question: they show that what was interpreted as Gnosticism in the Gospel is really a dualism (light against darkness), which we find current in Palestine at the time of Christ, and which is exemplified both in the scrolls and in the New Testament. The striking parallels between the Qumran scrolls and the writings of St. John give strong proof of the Palestinian background and origins of the latter. One who reads the scrolls and St. John together has the feeling that the authors belong to the same world, that St. John "speaks the language" of the desert dwellers of Qumran. We will summarize here the points that bear on the writings of St. John:

1. A dominant note in the Qumran theology is what is called dualism—the idea that the world is ruled by two powers, one good and one evil. Because the Qumran sources explicitly state that God *created* both, this is a modified dualism; both are subject to Him (1QS 3:25). The good spirit

is named in the scrolls: the spirit of truth, the angel of his (God's) truth, the prince of lights (1QS 3:18–24). Opposed to him is Belial (1QS 1, *passim*), who also has other names: the spirit of perversity and the angel of darkness (1QS 3:19–21; cf 1QM 17:5–6). These very titles show that the themes of light-darkness and truth-perversity are practically interchangeable in the Qumran writings.

2. God had divided mankind into two groups, each headed by the spirits, and between them is implacable hostility. The spirits fight for control of man's heart (1QS 3:20–21). Those who do good are in the hands of the prince of lights; those who do evil are in the hands of the angel of darkness. Thus a note of determinism is established, although it is not simply to be concluded that freedom of the will is denied. The typical Old Testament point of view is to disregard secondary causes and consider God the cause of everything, and it is this aspect which colors the Qumran teaching. The Qumranites never posed the problem of freedom of the will, just as it is never discussed in the Old Testament. But they do heap blame upon those who do wrong; they speak of man's "rejection" of God's teaching (1QS 3:1) and they recognize degrees of guilt in sin (1QS 5:11).

3. The lines are drawn between those who do good and those who do evil; they are engaged in a great struggle which will last until the "final period" (1QS 4:17), a "season of visitation," in which God will determine the lot of man according to the spirit in him. He will do away with sin and light will triumph over darkness. The people of Qumran felt that this final period was not far distant, and their War scroll seems to be a description of the glorious victory in the final battle. The "saints" of Qumran identified themselves as the "witnesses of truth" (1QS 8:6) and the "children of light" (1QS 1:9). They alone are the community chosen by God (1QS 8:6), whereas all outside their group belong to Belial. Hence there is sworn enmity against all outsiders (and this would naturally include other Jews): "hate all the children of darkness, each according to his guilt which God will avenge" (1QS 1:10). This is one reason for their withdrawal from the world to a place where they can "do the truth" with God; they are never to reveal to outsiders the Qumran interpretation of the Law (1QS 9:17–18). On the other hand, among themselves there is to prevail the greatest charity (e.g., 1QS 8:2–3).

4. Springing from this opposition are the two "ways" pursued by mankind, which is under the

dominion of the spirits. The way of the spirit of truth is described in the Manual of Discipline, 4:2–9:

to illuminate man's heart and make straight before him all the paths of true justice; to put in his heart fear of God's laws; a humble spirit and patience, abundant mercy and eternal goodness; discernment and understanding and valiant wisdom which believes in God's actions and relies on His abundant grace; a spirit of knowledge in every deliberate deed, and a zeal for just laws, a holy purpose with firm intent, abundant mercy for all the children of truth and a glorious purity which loathes all unclean idols; a humble conduct with all prudence and a faithful keeping secret the mysteries of knowledge; these are the counsels of the spirit for the children of truth . . . (1QS 4:2–6).

To the wicked spirit there belongs:

a haughtiness of soul and laziness in performing justice, iniquity and lies, arrogance and pride of heart, lying and deceit, cruelty and much lawlessness, short temper and much foolishness, eager insolence, loathesome deeds in a lustful spirit and unclean conduct enslaved to impurity, and a blasphemous tongue, blind eyes and dull ears, a stiff neck and dull heart, so that one walks in all the paths of darkness and evil scheming . . . (1QS 4:9–11).

There seem to be two meanings to the word "spirit" as it is used in the Qumran sources; it stands both for the opposing "angels" as well as for the influence which they initiate and exert in the heart of man. When a novice applies for membership in the community he is to be examined with regard to his spirit; is there in him the spirit of light or darkness, truth or perversity? His conduct will reveal the answer (1QS 5:20–24; 6:17–21).

This brief characterization of Qumran dualism will suffice for a comparison with St. John. It is not difficult to see a tremendous chasm between the Joannine message of Christianity and this narrow sectarian view. The difference is, of course, Christ. The specific Christian revelation—God's sending His only-begotten Son into the world to teach and to redeem mankind by His death—is simply not found in Qumran. But *the form of expression* of many elements in the Joannine writings is remarkably similar to the Qumran point of view.

1. Jesus is not only the Logos, or Word (Jn. 1:1), but He is also the Light who has come into the world (Jn. 1:4,9; 12:46)—as Jesus described

himself to the Pharisees, "the light of the world" (8:12). The light that Qumran hankered after was all the time in Palestine; it was not a created spirit, but the Son of God! Opposed to the Light is Satan, "the prince of this world" (Jn. 12:31), but he has no claim on Jesus (Jn. 14:30–31). Although St. John never directly defines Satan in terms of darkness, one would not be unfaithful to Joannine thought to say that for him Satan is the angel of darkness (just as Jesus speaks of the "power of darkness" in Lk. 22:53).

2. To Jesus has been given "power over all mankind" (Jn. 17:2); His Father has "given all things into His Hand" (Jn. 3:35; 13:3). He reminds His Apostles that it is He who has chosen them (Jn. 15:16), and it is the Father who has drawn them (Jn. 6:44). But along with what seems like a tinge of determinism is the free invitation: "A little while longer will the light be among you. Walk while you have the light, or darkness will overtake you. He who walks in darkness does not see where he is going" (Jn. 12:35). St. John is fond of drawing the lines between those who truly belong to Christ and those who do not. The children of God will not sin because they have in themselves a germ of life implanted by God (1 Jn. 3:9). On the other hand, the devil has his children: those who commit sin (1 Jn. 3:8, 10).

3. For St. John, too, there is a struggle between light and darkness, but with a profound difference from Qumran: the tide has already turned; victory has been won. Jesus described himself as the light that came into the world, (Jn. 12:46), because He cast out the prince of this world (Jn. 12:31), "rescuing us from the power of darkness," as St. Paul described it (Col. 1:13). Therefore, the Christian, unlike the Qumranite, is not to separate himself from the world, although it hates him; but Jesus prays that his disciples will be preserved from the world's evil influence (Jn. 17:14–16). The ultimate triumph for his followers, then, will not be that of light over darkness, but the *Parousia,* the second coming of Christ, for which the early Church yearned.

4. The light-darkness metaphor also applies to the "way" of mankind: "As long as you have the light, believe in the light, that you may become children of light" (Jn. 12:36). For St. John it is belief in Christ that makes one a child of light, not the observance of the Mosaic Law. St. Paul describes the commission he received from Jesus at the time of his conversion: "to open their eyes that they may turn from darkness to light and from the dominion of Satan to God" (Acts 26:18). Unfortunately, some loved the darkness more than the light: "This is how the sentence of condemnation

is passed: the light has come into the world, but men loved the darkness more than the light, because their lives were bad. Only an evildoer hates the light and refuses to face the light, for fear his practices may be exposed" (Jn. 3:19–20). Walking in darkness is incompatible with union with Christ (1 Jn. 1:6).

For St. John, the touchstone by which one discovers those who are the children of God or the children of the devil is the failure to "do justice," which he explains as a failure to love the brethren (1 Jn. 3:10). He is constantly emphasizing mutual love, even though he never explicitly extends the precept of charity beyond the members of the Church. Such an extension he would have learned from the parable of the Good Samaritan, but St. John is so filled with the idea of Christ in His members, that he stays within that point of view. In the Manual of Discipline, as we have seen, there is likewise a consistent stress on love of the brethren; time after time the precept is given, and the similarity with St. John's command (which was the command of Jesus), is indeed striking. But the other side of the coin is that the Qumran teaching couples with the precept a shrill denunciation of all who do not belong to the community; these are to be hated (1QS 1:4; 9:21–22, etc.).

Since the children of darkness were ruled by the

evil spirit, one who applied for membership in the community had to be investigated. St. John also recommends a testing of spirits (1 Jn. 4:1–6). In this context he is speaking of false prophets, those who think the spirit of God is in them, inspiring and guiding their teaching. There is a simple test for determining if this is so. The spirit of God is recognized by what the prophet proclaims: the spirit of God professes that the incarnate Jesus has come from God. The spirit that is not from God, the spirit of Anti-Christ, can be known because it does not profess this Jesus.

The world of light-darkness and truth-perversity is to be found in St. Paul also. The Apostle never tired of reminding Christians of their dignity as children of light: "For you are all children of the light and children of the day. We are not of night, nor of darkness. Therefore, let us not sleep . . . For they who sleep, sleep at night . . . But let us, who are of the day, be sober . . ." (1 Thes. 5:5–8). And again, "for you were once darkness, but now you are light in the Lord. Walk, then, as children of light, for the fruit of the light is in all goodness and justice and truth . . . and have no fellowship with the unfruitful works of darkness . . ." (Eph. 5:8–11; cf Rom. 13:12).

We have already noted that truth and perversity are interchangeable with light and darkness in

Qumran terminology. In St. John's writings, the spirit of truth means the Third Person of the Blessed Trinity. Jesus is the Light, his Spirit is the Spirit of Truth, who proceeds from the Father and bears witness to Jesus, and will teach all truth (Jn. 14:16–17; 15:26; 16:13). There is no opposing "spirit of perversity," but the equivalent is there: Satan, the father of lies (Jn. 8:44). Just as there is a reaction to the Light, so there is a reaction to Truth, in both Qumran and Christianity. One *does* the truth; whenever the Manual of Discipline uses this phrase, it is in an enumeration of the ideals of the community: justice, devotion, humility (1QS 1:5; 5:3; 8:2). For St. John, one who does the truth has performed his actions "in God" (Jn. 3, 21). Again, "walking in darkness" is the same as "not doing the truth" (1 Jn. 1:6; see also 3 Jn. 3).

The role assigned to truth in Qumran and in St. John is strikingly similar. The Manual of Discipline describes God's visitation in the final period:

Then God will purify by His truth all the actions of man and cleanse for Himself some of mankind so as to remove every evil spirit from his flesh, and to purify man by a holy spirit from all wicked deeds; and he will sprinkle upon him a spirit of truth like purifying water that cleanses from every lying abomination, and from wallow-

ing in an unclean spirit—to make the just com-
prehend knowledge of the Most High and to
make those who are perfect in conduct understand the wisdom of the sons of heaven (1QS
4:20–22).

One is reminded of the sacerdotal prayer in St.
John, 17:17–19, where Jesus asks His Father to
sanctify His disciples "in truth," for the Father's
word is truth. Moreover, just as the truth in the
Qumran text has a sanctifying effect, it is truth
that sets man free (Jn. 8:32–36). Freedom from
what? From the dominion of Satan, the father of
those who sin. Again, this Qumran text indicates
that the result of God's sprinkling the spirit of truth
upon man will be to communicate "knowledge of
the Most High." Similarly, one of the functions
of the Spirit of Truth (i.e., the Holy Spirit) is to
guide the followers of Jesus in the way of truth
(Jn. 16:31; cf. 1 Jn. 2:27).

For many years scholars have discussed the
Logos doctrine of St. John and speculated about
the choice of this term, "Word," which has such
a rich connotation in both Jewish and Hellenistic
thought. Now a new and striking parallel to John
1:3 ("all things were made through him, and without him was made nothing that was made") is
afforded in the Qumran literature. In a poetical

section of the Manual of Discipline, the writer acclaims God's all-pervasive knowledge and causality:

> Right belongs to God,
> and from His hand comes perfect conduct;
> through His knowledge is everything made
> and everything that is, He establishes by His thought,
> and without Him nothing is made (1QS 11:10–11).

The Qumran writer goes back to the ultimate in explaining the divine causality in all matters: God's dominion over the world stems from the fact that He created all that exists—and by His knowledge, just as all things were created through the Word. Moreover, this is asserted in typical Semitic fashion, first positively and then negatively ("without him nothing"). St. John seems to be phrasing his message concerning the Second Person with an eye to God's causality as understood by his contemporaries. Both build upon Old Testament concepts (e.g., the personification of Wisdom in creation, as Proverbs 8, Sirach 24), but St. John could have found the Qumran formula ready to hand.

From this comparison of the writings of Qumran

and St. John, we may draw several conclusions. First, it is a mistake to consider St. John's theology as being *merely* a development of Qumran; despite a similarity of outlook, the message of St. John is too unique to be lumped together with Qumran. If we have not stressed the *significant differences* between Qumran and the Joannine writings, it is because there is no need to do so; they should be apparent to all who study the scrolls. The importance of the similarities is that they help us understand the infant Church in its Palestinian setting.

Second, the close parallelism in phraseology and ideas cannot be explained by mere coincidence or by the common source, the Old Testament. It is straining too much to imagine that St. John developed on his own some elementary notions of light and darkness which are found briefly in the Old Testament, while the Qumran community went through its own similar development in another corner and *in the same general period*. No, these Qumran concepts were current in the world that Jesus lived in (Josephus reminds us that the Essenes were in every city). The striking fact is that Jesus and the New Testament writers met the challenge of their times and developed those ideas, applying them in such a way that the message of

Christianity was expressed in current, meaningful terms, in a majestic sweep of phrase and concept that keeps its appeal even in modern times. The light which the new scrolls throw on the New Testament is a salutary reminder that Jesus did not speak in a vacuum, that He was very much aware of the religious ideas and aspirations of His contemporaries. While it is true that no teacher spoke as He did (Mk. 1:22), and also that He came to tell what He had heard from His Father (Jn. 15:15), it is equally true that He was in all things like unto His brethren (Heb. 2:17), even to His very speech.

Third, while the phraseology of Qumran and St. John have a striking similarity to each other, it is just as obvious that the specific theological content of most of the terms is different for each. The Qumranites still remain children of the Old Testament, attached to the Law of Moses. But for Christians, Christ is the Light of the World, not a created principle or angel; the spirit of truth is the Holy Spirit, the Third Person of the Blessed Trinity, and so on.

Fourth, the evidence that we have presented does not prove direct contact between St. John and the Qumran community. It is enough that these ideas were current. More than likely some of the early Christians were associated with the Essenes,

perhaps converts from Essenism. But it is guess-
work to make an erstwhile Essene out of St. John
the Evangelist, much less Jesus.

The Sermon on the Mount

One of the Gospel sections that can be most
copiously documented from Jewish sources is the
Sermon on the Mount. This is as we would expect
because on the occasion of this sermon Jesus de-
clared that his mission was not to annul but to ful-
fill the Law and the Prophets (Mt. 5:17). The
newly discovered scrolls are another Jewish source
that illustrates some of the sayings of Jesus.

In 1956 there was published the first announce-
ment of a Qumran text that was similar to the
"Beatitudes." Like the words of Our Lord in
Matthew 5:3ff., they begin "Blessed is the one who
. . ." There is nothing startling about this because
the formula is found already in many places in the
Old Testament (e.g., Ps. 1). But once more we
have an indication of the traditional Jewish phraseology on the lips of Jesus. Preliminary reports concerning the Qumran "Beatitude" fragments do not
claim that it is similar in content to the words of
Jesus; the text itself has not yet been published.

"You have heard it said: 'Love your neighbor,
and hate your enemy'" (Mt. 5:43). Where did

Jesus' audience hear this said? There is no command in the Old Testament that the Jews were to *hate* their enemies. But in the Qumran literature, such hatred is positively taught. The members of the community are bidden to "hate the children of darkness" (1QS 1:10). In the ceremony of entering the covenant, whereby one became a member of the community, the Levites pronounce curses upon the followers of Belial (1QS 2:5–9). Anyone outside the fold is the object of hatred; on the other hand, we have seen above that the greatest love for each other is commanded by the Qumran regulations.

"Blessed are the poor in spirit" (Mt. 5:3). Translators of the New Testament have found it difficult to convey the meaning of "poor in spirit," which is expressed merely as "poor" in the parallel passage in St. Luke (6:20). The "poor" are found in the Old Testament (the *"anawim"*) and described as being close to God. But what is the meaning of the qualification "in spirit?" This phrase occurs once in the War scroll:

And he will give to the weak-kneed the power to stand and to the afflicted, strength to bear their burden; by the poor in spirit . . . the hardened heart, and by the perfect in conduct will be destroyed all wicked nations (1QM 14:7).

Despite the lacuna in the text, it is clear that "poor in spirit" is parallel to "perfect in conduct." These are the weak and afflicted to whom God gives strength and courage. One might choose "gentle" and "meek" as synonyms for our phrase except that these words do not bring out this essential note: the poor in spirit are holy and obedient to God's laws. The Qumran phrase, being practically contemporary with Our Lord, deserves to be considered in the exegesis of Matthew 5:3. Closely allied to our phrase is another from the War scroll (11:9–10), the "stricken in spirit," which is parallel to the "poor" (*'ebyonim*). These are the poor who by God's help will defeat the forces of Belial—another indication of the almost completely religious meaning of the word, "poor."

"You have heard that it was said to the men of old . . ." (Mt. 5:21). These men of old, or "ancients," is a term that occurs frequently in the scrolls to indicate previous generations; we have here merely an illustration of a common and contemporary vocabulary.

"Any one who is angry with his brother is answerable to the court; anyone who says to his brother, 'you imbecile,' is answerable to the Supreme Council . . ." (Mt. 5:22). While there is no strict parallel to this in the Qumran legislation, it is interesting to note that the regimentation of

Qumran is suggested by the degrees of "court" and "Supreme Council." The Qumran organization consisted of priests, levites and lay people who were arranged in groups called "tens," "fifties," "hundreds," and "thousands." The supreme authority was in the hands of a Superintendent and a council of twelve laymen and three priests.

Closely related to the above passage is the doctrine of fraternal correction described in Matthew 18:15–17, which has a parallel in the Manual of Discipline, 5:24–6:1. Jesus says that a brother is to be corrected privately when he does wrong to another; if he does not listen, the correction is to be administered before one or two witnesses; if he pays no attention to them, the church is to be notified. According to the Manual of Discipline, one should correct one's brother the same day, but without anger or hatred. And one is forbidden to accuse a brother before the members without having had recourse to a reproof before witnesses. It is clear that there are three stages in the procedure outlined by Jesus and mentioned implicitly in the Manual. Jesus must have been referring to a practice that was substantially identical with that of the Qumranites.

There are several other comparisons that can be made between the doctrine of the Sermon on the Mount and the teachings of the Qumran community. There is no reason to dwell at length upon them, since they merely show how contemporary the message of Jesus was:

1. Jesus forbids looking at a woman with lustful intention (Mt. 5:28); the Qumran literature condemns "lustful eyes" (1QS 1:6; DD 3:2), and "lustful spirit" (1QS 4:10).

2. Jesus prohibits oaths (Mt. 5:33–37). The Qumranites forbid various oaths (DD 19:1ff; 20:2ff), although they pronounced a solemn oath when they entered the covenant. According to Josephus the Essenes forbade all swearing.

3. Jesus revokes the *lex talionis* and urges turning the cheek (Mt. 5:38–39). Similarly, the writer in 1QS 10:17–18 declares that he will not repay a person for evil, but will "pursue" him with good.

4. Jesus teaches that one cannot serve money and God (Mt. 6:24). A similar ideal pervades the community which calls itself "the poor."

Father Coppens of Louvain has pointed out three fundamental moral attitudes which are shared by Qumran and Christianity: a basic opposition to impurity, a marked hostility to riches, the ideal of brotherly love. But the New Testament ideal of moral perfection far transcends the Qumran teaching. Christian charity is not limited to the brethren; Christian virginity "for the sake of the kingdom of Heaven" (Mt. 19:12), is absent, if indeed celibacy was practiced at all at Qumran. Their teaching and practice of celibacy is not clear: married life is presupposed in the Damascus Document, but there is merely a passing reference to women in the Manual of Discipline. The differences might be summarized this way: Qumran lacks the spirit of sonship by which a Christian calls God his Father (Rom. 8:15), and the definition of God as Love (1 Jn. 4:16).

The Acts and Epistles

The Epistles of St. Paul and the other apostles are the outgrowth of the missionary activity of the early Church, which is described in the Acts of the Apostles. From these sources we learn of certain practices and aspects of the early Church which it will be instructive to compare with the Qumran community.

One of the strong impressions which the first chapters of Acts leaves with even a casual reader is the sense of the Church's unity—the unity for which Christ prayed (Jn. 17:21):

All the believers were united, and held all things in common. They would sell their possessions and goods and distribute them to everyone as need required. Daily with one accord they attended the temple, and breaking bread at their homes, took their food with gladness and simplicity of heart, praising God and having the good will of all the people (Acts 2:44–47).

When Peter and John had their first altercation with the temple authorities, they reported it to their companions and all prayed together:

the congregation of believers were of one heart and one soul. Not one of them claimed as his own anything he possessed. They held all things in common . . . No one among the faithful was in want. Those who owned land or houses would sell them and bring the price of what they sold and lay it at the feet of the apostles, who distributed to each according to his need (Acts 4:32–36).

The famous exception to this ideal of communal life is Ananias, who held back part of the money he had acquired from the sale of his land (Acts 5:1–11). The practice of holding things in common was apparently only a phase and a short-lived one, in the early Church which grew too fast for such a way of life to be practicable. However, St. Paul's repeated requests for donations to aid poor communities show that the ideal of sharing was never lost.

The unity of the Church finds a counterpart in the strong sense of oneness which bound the Qumranites. They were a *Yahad*, a (comm)unity, and this word runs through all their writings. Just as the early Church called itself "the elect," (Rom. 8:33) "the saints," (Acts 9:13) and "those who witness to the truth" (3 Jn. 3; and Jn. 18:37, where Jesus so describes himself), so also the Qumran community is referred to in the same way: "men of holiness" (1QS 8:23), "witnesses of truth," and "elect of grace," (1QS 8:6).

The Qumran spirit of unity is expressed even in their very buildings. Although they lived apart in caves and tents, they came together at the community center. There they prayed together, dined together, studied the holy books together. Moreover, they handed over their possessions to a common treasurer for the good of the community. The details concerning this common purse are not clear to us; actually, it appears that some private property also existed, since some of the penalties administered for infraction of rules demand a payment. But the general impression is that there was a common purse at Qumran.

One difference between Qumran and the early Church that will almost immediately strike the reader is the *voluntary* character of the Christian offering; in Acts 5:1–11 Ananias need not have turned any money in, even after selling the field. The common purse at Qumran is part of the strict regulations once one becomes a full-fledged member. One has the feeling that the spirit in each case is different. There are good reasons to think that the Christian communal way of life was influenced only in a very broad sense by the Essene practice. The Christian practice is an extension of the type of life led by Jesus and the Twelve. They, too, possessed things in common and had their "treasurer." This was not due to any prerequisite for membership; it was just that the practical necessities of their ministry would be better served. On the other hand, Jesus and the Twelve did not do something new and unheard of; manifestly, the Essenes about them were practicing this common life. The practice was doubtless widely known and could have been adopted by any group with a sense of dedication to a mission. In this sense, one may speak of Essene influence. But it is not likely that the early Christian community would have been so unrealistic as to consciously imitate the Essenes. They would hardly adopt a way of life that was feasible only for a small group that cut itself off from society; this was clearly unsuited to the policy of expansion adopted by the Christians. Their communal life is simply a transition phase; at first a closely-knit group, they lived in the manner of Jesus and the Twelve, mindful of Christ's emphasis on the danger of riches and the necessity of sacrifice. Without relinquishing the ideals stressed by Christ, their rapid expansion soon brought about the end of communal life.

St. Luke tells us that it was at Antioch that the disciples were first called Christians. But they had their own name for Christianity; it was the "Way." Three times St. Paul, speaking of his persecution of the Church, uses this word (Acts 9:2; 22:4; 24:14) and so does St. Luke (Acts 18:25; 19:9, 23). The term was consecrated by Old Testament usage in the sense of "conduct," and by Christ Himself who said He was the Way (Jn. 14:6). It is also a key word in the Qumran literature: the spirit of truth and the spirit of perversity inspire the ways of good and wicked men in this world (1QS 3:18ff). The doctrine of the two ways is the familiar modified dualism which we have discussed above in relation to St. John's writings. But the New Testament dualism is not the same as the usage of the term "way" as a synonym for Christianity. As a synonym, the word has no dualistic connotation; it is simply a metaphorical usage to indicate a mode of life. Essentially the same metaphor is used frequently in both the Old and New Testament, where "way" is practically the equivalent of "conduct." Since there is as yet no evidence that the Essenes called their religion the "Way," the Christian usage is best explained from the common religious terminology of the day without any specific Qumran influence.

There are two terms describing the organization of the Qumran community that find an echo in the organization of the early Church: the *mebaqqer,* or New Testament *episkopos* (superintendent), and the *rabbim* or New Testament *plethos* (Many). Unfortunately, it is not clear from our texts whether there are one or many superintendents; the sources speak of the superintendent of all the camps, the camp superintendent and the superintendent of the Many. It seems best to assume that all these functions were part of the office of superintendent. This man presides over the Many and examines and instructs candidates who apply for membership in the community (1QS 6:12ff). The Damascus Document (17:6) determines that he is to be from thirty to fifty years of age. He is to instruct the Many and act towards them like a father and shepherd, and he has supreme authority in regulating the dealings of the community with outsiders (16:1–8). The corresponding Greek term *episkopos* designates the head of a particular Church in the New Testament. To the presbyters, or elders, who gathered to meet St. Paul at Miletus on his last trip to Jerusalem, the Apostle gives the name *episkopoi;* they are the superintendents who shepherd God's Church (Acts 20:28). Not only is there an etymological correspondence between the Qumran and Christian official, their *functions* were similar, even if we allow for the specific characteristics of the Christian *episkopos*. It is most probable that the early Christian community was aware of the hierarchical structure of the Essenes (and perhaps of other groups of which we are ignorant). They must have been influenced by such a social pattern, although there is the Old Testament ideal of the shepherd (Is. 40:11; Ez. 34:12) which nourished both groups, and the Christians never forgot Jesus' words about the Good Shepherd (Jn. 10).

The recognition of the pre-Christian origin of the office of Superintendent will have an effect on the dating and authorship of the Pastoral Epistles (Titus, 1 and 2 Timothy). It can no longer be argued that the ecclesiastical organization shown in these Epistles is too advanced for the age of St. Paul; the Qumran organization shows that there were historical antecedents for Christianity to imitate.

A frequent word in the Qumran literature is *harabbim,* or "the Many," which is a technical term for the general body of the members. It occurs most often in the legislative passages (e.g., 1QS 6 and DD 15), where penalties are assigned for various disorders which may occur during the assemblies of the Many. The Many are distinguished from the ruling council and from the "novices" who are on probation; they are the full-fledged members. In the New Testament, *plethos* corresponds to *rabbim,* first of all in the general sense of multitude, such as the multitude of the heavenly host that appeared to the Bethlehem shepherds (Lk. 2:13). But it also has a more limited meaning. In Acts 6:2 the Twelve summon the Many (*plethos*) and propose to them the selection of deacons; in 6:5, the Many signify their approval. At the Jerusalem Council (Acts 15:12), it is said that "all the Many" listened to Paul and Barnabas speak. The deliberations of this council are then sent by letter to the "Many" at Antioch (Acts 15:30), who joyfully accept them. The analogy between the Many in these New Testament passages and in the Qumran writings is unmistakable; in both the members of a society are designated. Nevertheless, the use of Many in this technical sense is relatively infrequent in the New Testament; *ekklesia* or "church" occurs far more often. The fact that the term "Many" is used at all may be due to Palestinian sources which St. Luke was using for the history of the Jerusalem Church;

and it is likely that the Qumran term had become part of the general vocabulary of the period.

There are several passages in the Pauline epistles that echo Qumran phraseology and ïdeas. We have quoted above some examples of the familiar dualism (1 Thes. 5:5–8; Eph. 5:8–11). Another striking example is 2 Corinthians 6:14–17, where St. Paul advises the Corinthians not to associate with pagans. "What has holiness in common with iniquity? Or what fellowship has light with darkness? What agreement is there between Christ and Beliar? Or what part has the believer with the unbeliever?" This is the only time that Beliar or Belial (an Old Testament term, "Good for Nothing") is mentioned, and practically every metaphor in these verses can be matched with a quotation from Qumran (see 1QS 3). There can be no doubt that Paul is adapting Essene terminology to his own ends, whether he was conscious of it or not. The same observation can be made of Colossians 1:12–14, where he speaks of the Father "who has qualified you for a share in the lot of the saints in the light and who has rescued us from the power of darkness, and transferred us into the kingdom of his beloved Son, in whom we have our redemption, the remission of our sins." This is a succinct statement of redemption by Christ, expressed in characteristically Qumran language:

lot, saints, light, power of darkness (e.g., 1QS 11:7–8).

When St. Paul speaks of the Christian's struggle against the powers of evil, he describes the Principalities and Powers as "those who rule the world of darkness" (Eph. 6:12), much as the Manual of Discipline conceives of "the dominion of Belial" (1QS 2:19), under whom "the spirits of darkness" (1QS 3:25) operate. Paul urges his readers whom he has called "the children of light" (Eph. 5:8) to take up the shield of faith against the "flaming arrows of the wicked enemy" (Eph. 6:16), while the Qumran psalmist also speaks of the "arrows of the pit" (1QH 3:27) which the wicked have inflicted upon him.

One of the key words in the Pauline Epistles is the word *musterion*, or mystery. He speaks in Ephesians 1:9–10 of the mystery of God's will, namely that Christ is supreme over all. The mystery that is Christ was kept hidden from eternity in God (Eph. 3:9; see Rom. 16:25; 1 Cor. 2:7; Col. 1:25–27), but now it is revealed to mankind. This same word, *raz*, or mystery (sometimes *sod*, meaning "hidden counsel"), runs through the scrolls as well as through the later Jewish apocryphal literature. In the scrolls the term refers to the destiny God has determined for the world and man, the hidden decrees which the community alone has been given to know. The Manual of Discipline speaks of "the mysteries of knowledge" (4:6), i.e., the Qumran teachings which the community is to keep hidden from outsiders; these are the mysteries of God's understanding (4:18), by which He has determined the battle and ultimate victory of light over darkness (see also 11:3–6). Like the mysteries of which Paul speaks, these mysteries too, show forth God's power and glory and have been revealed to his servants, the prophets. The point to be emphasized here is that Paul is using a terminology that is allied to the Qumran usage and which is to be found in other apocryphal literature of the period. But in the Epistles it has a specific Christian content that really transforms the word itself.

The Jewish doctrine of justification was characterized by "works," by the observance of the Law. Paul's antithesis between faith in Christ and the performance of the precepts of the Law is well known (e.g., Rom. 3:21–22). One does not attain justification by the works of the Law, but by faith in Christ. It is interesting to note how close to this the Qumran teaching is. In one of the Thanksgiving Psalms (4:30–33), the author complains that man is guilty from his birth to his death:

I know that man has no right,
the son of man, no perfect conduct;

to God Most High belongs all just deeds,
and man's conduct is not made firm
except by the spirit which God has created for
    him,
to make perfect the conduct of the sons of men
so that they know all He has done by His mighty
    power
and His copious mercy for the children of His
    favor.

The hymn with which the Manual of Discipline closes expresses the same reliance upon God, the same impotence of man:

As for me, my right is God's,
in His hand is my perfect conduct
and my just heart;
and by his justice is my wrong wiped out . . .
If I begin to fall,
God's love is my salvation forever;
if I stumble by sinful human weakness,
my right will stand forever because of God's
    justice . . . (1QS 11:10–12)

This deep sense of human guilt and unworthiness is entirely in the tradition of the Old Testament Psalms (23, 42, 51, 73; Hebrew numbering). Yet the Qumranites are very close to the ideas of the

New Testament. Even if their words are tinged with their fatalistic doctrines, there is no denying that they prepare the way for the Christian idea of justification through Christ. Humanity is morally bankrupt and justification can come only from God, says Qumran; and St. Paul specifies, "in Christ." The remarkable fact is that these ideas were circulating in Palestine when Christianity was born. So much emphasis has been laid upon the doctrine of the Pharisees about the works of the Law, against which St. Paul had to write, that the other side of the picture, now presented by the recent discoveries, is altogether new and surprising.

Jesus and the Teacher of Righteousness

In the popular mind a correlation between Qumran and Christianity has been made that is not true, and which does a disservice to the scrolls by a false emphasis. We have seen abundant evidence of the light they throw on New Testament ideas and practice. But they do not give evidence of a "Christianity before Christianity," or evidence that Christianity is an Essenism. By a false emphasis upon the Qumran teacher of righteousness, the true value of the scrolls is neglected and passed over by many moderns. The alleged parallel between the teacher and Jesus has been popularized in the work of Edmund Wilson and the eminent French scholar, A. Dupont-Sommer. The latter claimed that Christ now appears in many ways as an "astonishing reincarnation of the teacher of righteousness." This was a most unfortunate and misleading development in the study of the scrolls. In view of Dupont-Sommer's clarification in the *Saturday Review* for March 3, 1956, it is evident that he does not deny the uniqueness of Christ on the basis of the scrolls; moreover he admits that they offer no challenge to the general originality of the Christian Church.

How was it possible that this relationship ("reincarnation") between the teacher and Jesus could be asserted in the first place? It was because of the over-enthusiastic interpretations and faulty translations of Dupont-Sommer; so hypnotized was he by his own theory that he read it into the holes of the leather of the Habacuc commentary. It is not to be denied that there are some valid, even if superficial, resemblances between the two; both the teacher and Jesus taught lofty moral ideals and both were persecuted; faith in both was demanded of their followers (the coloring of the word "faith" seems to be that of observance of the teacher's doctrine rather than personal devotion to him; nowhere in the Qumran texts is personal loyalty to the teacher asked of the members). In many points there is a similarity between the religious ideas and beliefs expressed in the Qumran scrolls and those of the New Testament, as we have seen. But Dupont-Sommer went far beyond this. For him the teacher is recognized as the Messiah, the "Redeemer of the World," a divine being whose sufferings resemble that of Jesus and influenced the composition of the "Servant of the Lord" poems in the second part of the book of Isaias. Let us look at the evidence for these claims.

1. Was the teacher recognized by his followers as the Messiah? It would not be surprising if this had been so, since there were several claimants to this title before and after the time of Christ. But there is no evidence that the teacher was regarded as the Messiah; in fact, the evidence is against it. The Messianic beliefs of the community turn out to be extremely complex. They believe that three figures will play a role in the Messianic era: a prophet and two Messiahs. The two Messiahs are those of Aaron (a priestly Messiah) and of Israel (a royal, Davidic Messiah). These Messianic ideas are clearly seen in the fragments of two columns belonging to the Manual of Discipline, which were published in 1955; here the Messiah shares in the community's banquet, but plays a role subordinate to the officiating priest. There is nothing in the Messianic teaching of the scrolls that would in-

dicate that the teacher is to be identified with either of these figures.

2. Who applies the title "Redeemer of the World" to the teacher? So far this has not been found in any of the scrolls or fragments. The phrase does occur in the apocryphal work, the Testaments of the Twelve Patriarchs, (Testament of Levi, chapters 10 and 14), and Dupont-Sommer claims that it refers to the teacher, but no convincing proof has been given. A major objection to his procedure is the undisputed fact that later, Christian, interpolations and changes have been made in the text of the Testaments; the phrase "Redeemer of the World," is to be regarded as one of these. Moreover, the concept of a suffering Messias who redeems the world is one that not even the followers of Christ readily accepted. Jesus had to explain the prophecies of the Old Testament to Cleopas and the other disciple whom He met on the way to Emmaus: "Was it not necessary that the Messias should undergo these sufferings and thus enter into his glory?" (Lk. 24:26; see also 18:31–34). The fact is that the world in which our Lord lived was not prepared for a crucified "Redeemer of the World."

3. Is the teacher a "divine being?" The Habacuc commentary is made to yield phrases that are reminiscent of the passion of Jesus; thus in 11:6

the wicked priest dared to strip the teacher of his clothes. Thanks to the discovery of a papyrus in the Wadi Murabbaat cache, it is certain that this phrase cannot be so translated. It is now correctly rendered "in the place of his (the teacher's) exile." But the *pièce de résistance* is to be found in 8:16–9:2 of the Habacuc commentary where the author, commenting on Habacuc 2:7–8, says:

> . . . (con)cerning the priest who rebelled . . . to strike him with wicked judgments. Horrible evil diseases they inflicted upon him, and vengeance on the body of his flesh.

Dupont-Sommer is clairvoyant in his comment on the passage:

> This passage evidently alludes to the passion of the teacher of righteousness; he was judged, condemned, punished: He suffered "in his body of flesh"; doubtless he was a divine being who "became incarnate" to live and die as a man.

The phrase "body of flesh" does not give the slightest suggestion of a divine being; it occurs in Sirach 23:16, referring to a wicked man, and in Colossians 2:11, referring to a Christian. Finally and most importantly, who is suffering? Due to a lacuna in the text, the sufferer is not identified, but the person mentioned previous to the lacuna is "the priest who rebelled." It is Dupont-Sommer who has proposed a change of subject in the space that is missing so that he refers the suffering to the teacher. But the tenor of the passage suggests the contrary. Since Habacuc 2:7–8, which is being commented upon, refers to an unjust, greedy person who is to be repaid for his plundering and bloodshed, the passage of the commentary should be understood of the punishment of the rebellious priest and not the teacher.

4. Are the sufferings of the Servant in the second part of Isaias (52–53), a reflection of the sufferings of the teacher? The evidence for this is extremely tenuous in itself; it rests on the alleged Messianic references in chapters 52–53 of the Isaias scroll, which the Qumranites are supposed to have made more pronounced in view of their teacher. The arguments against such a haphazard composition of this part of Isaias are quite strong: arguments of style and content which fit the suffering Servant songs into the framework of the exilic and immediate post-exilic period. In our present state of knowledge, the passion and death of the teacher of righteousness is a myth. He was persecuted by the wicked priest (perhaps Alexander Jannaeus); that much we know. Only two

texts speak of his death, and both in an incidental way. The Damascus Document speaks of a time "from the day that the teacher of the community was gathered in until a Messiah arises from Aaron and Israel" (9:29). The same document mentions an interval of forty years "from the day that the teacher of the community was gathered in." The word that is used here, "gathered in," strongly suggests a natural, rather than a violent, death; it is the Hebrew term used in Genesis to describe the death of the patriarchs, Abraham, Isaac and Jacob. As a matter of fact, violent death for the teacher, even his crucifixion, would not be very surprising to us, because we know that crucifixion was practiced. But there is not even a hint of this in the texts that have been published.

5. The Habacuc commentary, 11:4–8, forms the basis of the alleged resurrection and return of the teacher. We have already seen that verses 4–6 state that the wicked priest persecuted the teacher "in the place of his exile." The next two verses go on to say that "he" appeared to "them" on their Sabbath rest:

Its explanation (of Habacuc 2:15) concerns the wicked priest who persecuted the teacher of righteousness, swallowing him up (or: leading him astray) in his sore wrath, in the place of his exile. At the time of the feast of Rest, on the Day of Atonement, he appeared to them, to swallow them up (or: lead them astray), and make them stumble on the day of Fast, their Sabbath Rest.

The normal sequence would presuppose that "he" refers to the previous subject, the wicked priest, and that "them" refers to the partisans of the teacher; it is thus that the majority of scholars understand the passage. Dupont-Sommer, however, interprets this to mean that the "glorious teacher," who had previously been put to death, now "shone forth" to punish Jerusalem for its crimes. There is no denying the contention of Dupont-Sommer that the verb *YP‘* ("appear, shine forth") is used in the theophanies of Yahweh in the Old Testament. But the word is also used of a wicked man! Therefore it does not always connote the appearance of a divine being. In the Hebrew fragments of Sirach the word occurs in 12:15, "while you stand firm, he (the proud or wicked man) makes no bold move (*lo yophia‘*—does not manifest himself); but if you slip, he cannot hold back." Likewise, the Damascus Document uses the word about the manifestation of wicked deeds (9:31, 33). There is no philological argument that demands Dupont-Sommer's "apotheosis" in this passage of the Habacuc commentary. Rather, it is the wicked priest who *appears* and afflicts the good people on the Day of Atonement. It may be said that the Qumranites looked forward to the return of the teacher in the "end-time," just as the resurrection of the just is described in the book of Daniel, but this is not a parallel to the resurrection of Jesus.

As one looks back on the Dupont-Sommer exegesis, it may seem surprising that it received so much attention. But the sensational has its appeal, and in this case it was accompanied by French style and clarity, not a few contributions by Dupont-Sommer himself to other phases of the scrolls, and by the authority of a competent linguist. But his airy parallels may be relegated to the limbo of abortive theories.

Conclusion

One cannot bring to a close this brief consideration of the scrolls and the Bible without emphasizing that not all the scrolls and fragments have as yet been published. The picture that has been sketched is necessarily incomplete and it may need revision in the light of future publications. We need to confess our ignorance, even as the curtain is raised on a new horizon. At the present time some "conclusions" are little more than hypotheses; many essential questions remain unanswered. For example, we have no consistent picture of the Essenism with which the Qumran community is generally identified. Did the community develop its own teaching over the long period of time that it settled at Qumran? What relationship does it have to the groups that, as Josephus tells us, settled in the cities? What is the relationship of the apocryphal writings, some fragments of which have been found in the caves, to the Qumran teachings? Despite the detailed knowledge we obtain from the Qumran scrolls, a complete picture of the community still eludes us.

Serious errors are built on arguments from silence. Because an ancient source does not speak, we may not conclude that it has nothing to say. The Qumran sources broke the silence which surrounded the religious background of the time of Christ. Yet they will raise almost as many questions as they settle. Caution is a necessity in reconstructing this historical period. We must expect varying degrees of probability rather than certainty in our conclusions.

The similarities between certain ideas in the New Testament and in the Qumran literature are surely not to be denied. It is true that in some alleged instances the similarities do not exist, but erroneous exaggerations are relatively easy to apprehend and dismiss. Similarity itself allows of degrees, and the most deceiving of these is verbal similarity. The same words may be used, but have a quite different meaning in Christianity than they had in the framework of the Qumran doctrine. For example, the angels' message in Luke 2:14 is peace to "men of good will." The equivalent Semitic phrase is to be found in one of the Qumran Thanksgiving Psalms (4:32–33), where the writer speaks of God's mercies being poured out upon "the children of his favor." In the Qumran text, God's favor is to be understood in the light of their teaching about God's will; the divine will predestines and determines man's action. Those who have entered the covenant of the community are called "the chosen of (God's) favor" (1QS 8:6). While the specific Qumran meaning is not present in St. Luke, there is a similarity; for St. Luke the Incarnation is God's predetermined plan for the "men of good will."

Practically all scholars agree that there is no direct literary dependence of the New Testament upon Qumran literature. In the New Testament we find clear allusions to some apocryphal works, as was recognized long before 1947 (e.g., the Assumption of Moses and the book of Enoch in the Epistle of Jude), and we know that these apocryphal works were popular among the Essenes. However, there is no specific Qumran source that is imitated or quoted in the New Testament.

Yet there can be no doubt that Jesus and the New Testament writers were acquainted with the Qumran teachings. It is difficult to determine the manner in which they came into contact with the Qumran doctrine. Some scholars would hold that St. John the Baptist and his former disciple, St. John the Evangelist, were members of the Essenes. As we have indicated above, there is just no evidence for this, despite the clear influence which the Qumran teachings exerted on both men. Other scholars have proposed that the Essenes were among the early converts to Christianity; this is entirely probable in view of the aspirations of these Jews. Their noble ideals, their asceticism, and their Messianic consciousness would have rendered them particularly susceptible to the appeal of Christianity. But this view, too, remains an assumption. I am inclined to think that the influence of Qumran upon Christianity was largely in an indirect manner: these Essene teachings were part of the general religious trend into which Christianity was born. The Qumran point of view was a climate more in accord with Christian ideals than was the official Judaism which outlawed the Essenes. Being part of the religious heritage of the first generation of Christians, it contributed to their fund of religious languages and ideas. The Christians could have adopted Qumran phraseology and practice without even being conscious of the fact that these "belonged" to that sect. The Essene teaching was so much a part of first century Judaism that it is as natural for Christianity to be affected by it as by the Old Testament religion in general. Moreover, it was just one of many currents, one tributary in the entire flood of religious ideas in the first century. It would be a mistake to forget that the contemporary influences on Christianity were on a broader basis than Qumran Essenism, and that the Essenes themselves drew on these many currents for their tenets and practices.

It should be remembered, moreover, that the New Testament writers were influenced in varying and unequal ways by Qumran Judaism. The most conspicuous affinity is found in the writings of St. John, next in certain epistles of St. Paul (Ephesians, Corinthians, Colossians), then in St. Matthew and St. Luke. Across the entire New Testament the voice of Qumran resembles the "still small voice" that Elias heard. We can be grateful that archeology has enabled this voice to be heard, because far from levelling the Christian Gospel, it will by contrast show forth the incomparably richer message that is Christ.

Dead Sea Diary

Spring, 1947:

Discovery of Cave 1, with its scrolls and jars, by Muhammad adh-Dhib.

July, 1947:

Syrian Archbishop Mar Yeshue Samuel buys some of the scrolls from the Bedouin for what is reported to be $150.

November – December, 1947:

Professor E. L. Sukenik of the Hebrew University in Jerusalem buys jars and other scrolls from Bethlehem antiquities dealer.

January – February, 1948:

Sukenik realizes the value of his scrolls. Having learned of the existence of the rest with the Archbishop, he made contact with the Syrians and even copied out columns of the complete Isaias scroll. But before any arrangements could be concluded (conditions in Palestine were in upheaval, due to Arab-Israeli battles), the Syrians had turned to the American School of Oriental Research in Jerusalem. They assured the Archbishop about the phenomenal acquisition he had made. During this year news of the scrolls was publicized throughout the world.

January 28, 1949:

A United Nations' officer, Philippe Lippens, and members of the Arab Legion rediscover Cave 1, and also the fact that it had been visited several times before them by clandestine diggers.

February 8 – March 5, 1949:

First scientific excavation of Cave 1, yielding about 600 fragments of seventy-five biblical and non-biblical works. Notable among these are parts of Leviticus in Phoenician script, which was used by the Jews before they adopted the Aramaic or "square" script in use today. Potsherds of jars and lamps, and the linen textiles in which the manuscripts were wrapped were unearthed and proved valuable for dating the age of the manuscripts.

November 24 – December 12, 1951:

First campaign of excavation at Khirbet Qumran, revealing a connection between Cave 1 (less than a mile to the north) and the Qumran ruins. Discovery of complete jar of same type as those found in cave, along with pottery and coins of first century A.D. Sections of the main building were uncovered and several rooms excavated; archeologists conclude that this was not a private dwelling, but a community center. Graves were opened, but no funeral offerings were found; the skeletons of men and women (no children) were buried in north-south direction.

At this point Bedouin start bringing in new material, claiming that it is from Cave 1, but in reality it is from the Wadi Murabbaat (18 kilometers south of Qumran).

January 21, 1952:

Six week dig begins at Wadi Murabbaat in four caves. Evidence of occupation in Chalcolithic, Middle Bronze II, Iron, and Roman periods. The texts, coming mostly from the second cave, are of varied types. There is a non-biblical document written in Hebrew on a papyrus palimpsest, dating perhaps from the seventh or sixth century B.C. From the first and second centuries A.D. are biblical fragments (Genesis, Exodus, Deuteronomy and Isaias) which are in agreement with the traditional Hebrew text. Also, a complete phylactery containing the four prescribed texts (Exodus, 8:1–10; 11–16; Deuteronomy, 11:13–21; 6:4–9), and several inscribed ostraca (potsherds); most notable of the last is a jar fragment with the first part of the Hebrew alphabet, each letter being written twice. A sensational discovery are the two letters signed by Simon ben Kosebah (Bar Kochba, famed leader in Second Jewish Revolt of 135 A.D.), to a certain Yeshua ben Gilgola, "chief of the camp." There are also matrimonial contracts in Greek (dating to 124 A.D.), a few small Latin fragments, and even some pieces with Arabic inscription.

None of these finds are to be connected with the Qumran community. The caves were military outposts during the war of Bar Kochba, which were overcome about 135 A.D., by the Roman army.

March 10–29, 1952:

Because the Bedouin kept bringing in new fragments purportedly found near Cave 1, the archeologists examine a five-mile radius about Khirbet Qumran, inspecting about forty caves. In twenty-five of them, they found typical Roman pottery of the kind discovered in Cave 1 and in the

Khirbet. Two caves (Cave 2 and Cave 3) contain fragments of manuscripts of the Hebrew Old Testament. In Cave 3 were discovered the two famous copper scrolls.

The March excavation had a resounding echo in September 22–29: the archeologists cleared Cave 4 which had been found and partially dug by the Bedouin; it contained fragments of over 300 distinct works, biblical and non-biblical.

Summer, 1952:

Bedouin bring in a new group of fragments from the Wadi en-Nar, about half-way between the Qumran and Murabbaat caves. First appearance of Greek New Testament works: fragments of Mark, John and Acts, that date from fifth to eighth century. In the Syro-Palestinian language are fragments of Luke, John, Acts and Colossians. In this area was also found an important Greek translation of the Minor Prophets. It is claimed by the Belgian campaign of 1953 that all these fragments come from Khirbet Mird.

February – April, 1953:

Major Lippens and Father de Langhe of Louvain, Belgium, excavate Khirbet Mird, the ruins of a Byzantine monastery located two and one-half miles northeast of Mar Saba in the Wadi en-Nar. The monastery is that of Castellion, on the site of ancient Hyrcania, the stronghold of John Hyrcanus. Yield: fragments of Greek New Testament texts, Syro-Palestinian and Arabic texts.

Spring, 1953, 1954, 1955, 1956:

Second, third, fourth, fifth (and perhaps final) campaign at Khirbet Qumran.

During 1955 and 1956, fragments were being brought to the authorities working in the Palestinian Museum, and money was raised to buy these. It is believed that virtually all fragments outstanding had been acquired in 1956.

Shortly before the 1956 compaign, Bedouin discovered Cave 11, from which they took several scrolls, as yet unidentified. Efforts are being made to recover these scrolls.

Appendix B

Genealogy of the Old Testament

Most of Hebrew Bible written and gathered into collections ("Law" and "Prophets"), copied and transmitted:

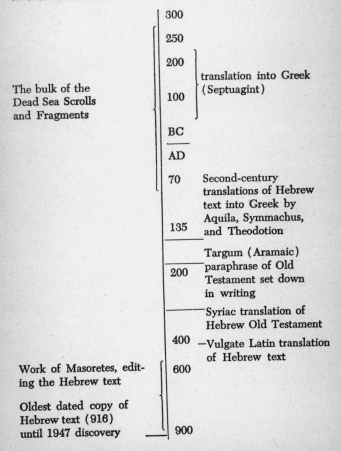

300

250

200   translation into Greek
                             (Septuagint)
100

The bulk of the
Dead Sea Scrolls
and Fragments

BC

AD

70   Second-century
            translations of Hebrew
            text into Greek by
            Aquila, Symmachus,
135   and Theodotion

            Targum (Aramaic)
200   paraphrase of Old
            Testament set down
            in writing

            Syriac translation of
            Hebrew Old Testament

400   Vulgate Latin translation
            of Hebrew text

Work of Masoretes, edit-   600
ing the Hebrew text

Oldest dated copy of
Hebrew text (916)
until 1947 discovery   900

A NOTE ON THE TYPE

IN WHICH THIS BOOK IS SET

This book is set in Caledonia, a Linotype face created in 1939 by W. A. Dwiggins, which is by far one of the best book types created in the last 50 years. It has a simple, hard-working, feet-on-the-ground quality and can be classed as a modern type face with excellent color and good readability. The designer claims Caledonia was created by putting a little of each of Scotch Roman, Bulmer, Baskerville and Bodoni together and producing a lively crisp-like book type. This book was composed by Progressive Typographers, York, Pa., and printed and bound by the Wickersham Printing Company, of Lancaster, Pa. The typography and design by Howard N. King.